WHEN GRACE COMES HOME

The Practical Difference That Calvinism Makes

Terry L. Johnson *Rom 11:36*

Christian Focus

© Terry L. Johnson
ISBN 185792 539 4

Published in 2000
by Christian Focus Publications,
Geanies House, Fearn, Ross-shire,
IV20 1TW, Great Britain

Cover design by Owen Daily

If anyone is foolish enough to think that theology, particularly Calvinistic theology, is impractical, he needs to read this book. And even if you don't, read it anyway. Terry Johnson has provided a splendid work on how right theology bears upon our worship, character, suffering, witness and growth in the Christian life. This is exactly what the evangelical church needs because, whether evangelicals know it or not, their future as a viable movement depends upon the rediscovery of such God-honoring theology.

Dr. James M. Boice
Tenth Presbyterian Church, Philadelphia

That 'grace reigns in righteousness' is a Pauline principle, unfortunately much-neglected in today's evangelical churches. Even in circles where 'Reformed theology' is unapologetically preached, one senses a general lack of corresponding experience. We may still teach 'the doctrines of grace', but we have given little thought to 'the practical implications of sovereign grace', or at least, we have not come to a unified view of what a robust biblical piety ought to look like. For this reason, and more, Terry Johnson's *When Grace Comes Home* is to be welcomed. He gives us, here, a biblical 'practical divinity'. In a day and age when many view 'Reformed Christianity' as a mere system of thought or worldview, rather than full-orbed expression of biblical religion, Johnson offers a helpful corrective. Until we are able to answer two questions: 'How does sovereign grace make a difference in life?' and 'How is sovereign grace making a difference in my life?' we are not yet 'Reformed'. So, may God grow you in grace, by His Spirit, as you study the biblical themes so faithfully expounded in this good book.

J. Ligon Duncan, III, PhD
Senior Minister, First Presbyterian Church, Jackson, Mississippi

'The fine book proves for Christians something that they should already know, but often miss: theology matters! With much practical wisdom and help for Christian thinking and living, this book makes good application of good theology.'

Rev. Dr. Robert Godfrey,
Westminster in California,

Terry L. Johnson is one of the rare Presbyterian ministers who is as concerned about Reformed practice as he is about Reformed theology. With this book, he enriches our understanding of the difference that the doctrines of grace not only make for the way we do theology, but also for the ways in which we serve God and love our neighbors. The Reformed tradition has too often been accused of being at best intellectual, at worst irrelevant. *When Grace Comes Home* proves that allegation false by showing that the best and most careful theology will inform even the most ordinary aspects of daily life.

D. G. Hart,
Westminster Theological Seminary, Philadelphia

Terry Johnson is representative of an important group of young theologians who are trying to recover classical Reformed Christianity. They are serious pastors who have seen through the pretentions of the liberal religious culture which dominated the twentieth century. They sense that in the past century too much of the fundamental genius of the Christian faith was given up and as a result the church has become vapid and ineffective. Here is a book which reaffirms the faith of the Reformation. One is not surprised to discover that the church which the author pastors is strong, healthy, and vibrant.

Hughes Oliphant Old

William Perkins once defined theology as 'the science of living blessedly for ever'. It is a good definition which combines two thoughts: that theology is a science, by which he meant that theology was capable of being measured and integrated into a coherent whole; and that the goal of theology is to enable Christians to live as God intends – comprehensively and intensively Christ-like. Theology – Reformed theology in particular – ought to make us more like Jesus. And that is what Terry Johnson's book does! He manages to make theology what it ought always to be: God-honouring and rigorously practical at the same time. Stressing the time-honoured value of the means of grace, this book urges Christians to grow in grace. A book we have needed for some time. I cannot recommend it too highly.

Dr. Derek W.H. Thomas
Reformed Theological Seminary,
Jackson, Mississippi

CONTENTS

PREFACE..7

INTRODUCTION...9

1. WORSHIP 19

2. HUMILITY 29

3. ADVERSITY 41

4. OUTLOOK 53

5. WITNESS 69

6. SANCTIFICATION 87

7. ASSURANCE 101

8. LAW AND LIBERTY 121

9. PRAYER 137

10. GUIDANCE 155

11. A FAITH FOR LIVING 169

INDICES 181

For Emily

PREFACE

A United States congressman recently noted that there are two kinds of political conservatives: those who are conservative and *glad* about it, and those who are conservative and *mad* about it. Glad? Oh yes, glad because of all the benefits they see coming from a conservative philosophy of government. Mad? Sorry, yes, there are those too. They are mad about the errant political opinions that are circulating and all the people who hold them. One should have no difficulty guessing which group is more effective in winning others to their point of view, the glad or the mad.

It seems that we have the same problem in the Christian world. There are Christians who are glad about being a Christian. They are overflowing with gratitude for all that they have in Christ. Then there are those who are mad. Their fundamental orientation is not the positive identity and benefits that they have in Christ, but anger at all those who don't share their outlook. They are Christian, but mad about it.

The doctrines of grace are something to be glad about. We readily admit that there are plenty of reasons for being mad. The world's philosophy destroys marriages, families, and communities. Its moral and religious relativism has broken down the marriage covenant, encouraged promiscuity, abortion, illegitimacy, single-parent households, and given us a generation of angry, alienated, and violent children. If one is a Reformed Christian there is additional material for anger coming out of the Christian community. How many people are robbed of their peace because other Christians persuade them they can have no eternal security? How many

are devastated by affliction because they've been taught that
God isn't sovereign? How many are trapped in the emotional
turmoil of unworkable 'higher life' views of sanctification?
When one soberly considers the net impact that deviant
philosophies and religions have upon human misery there is
much to be angry about. Yes there is, but should anger be our
dominant, our characteristic mood?

In our polemics with unbelievers and believers alike we
mustn't forget that the message of God's sovereign grace in
Christ is 'good news', it is gospel. The following book
attempts to demonstrate that believing those doctrines is
something to be glad about. In one practical area after
another, the message of grace fully understood takes us to the
highest heights of peace, comfort, thanksgiving, and joy that
it is possible to reach in this world. I invite you to walk along
those heights with me.

A word of caution before you proceed: even a book of
'practical divinity' needs to demonstrate its Biblical basis.
The first two chapters provide that basis, and for this reason
are a tougher read than the rest of the book. Persevere. They
are necessary if the rest is to have the impact that it should.
What impact? The impact for which I pray is that readers
would learn afresh the delights of the Reformed faith, that
they would be glad not mad, and more effective in bringing
others to the same convictions.

INTRODUCTION

Please read Romans 11:33-36

We are going to take a journey into the land of practical 'divinity,' as the old theologians called it. Specifically, we will endeavor to look at the practical difference the Calvinistic understanding of Biblical teaching makes. During our journey, I will use the designations 'Reformed' and 'Calvinistic' interchangeably with 'Biblical,' 'Bible-believing,' and 'Gospel,' for, like Spurgeon, I regard the former as synonymous with the latter. 'It is a nickname to call it Calvinism,' said Mr. Spurgeon, 'Calvinism is the gospel and nothing else.' You understand, then, that, for us, this is not a sectarian thing but a gospel thing. If you do not share this perspective, please do not take offense. Read on, we plead, for there is much here that we trust will be edifying for your soul as well.

What prompts us to begin this journey? Most of Protestantism looks back to founders who were essentially Calvinistic in their beliefs. This is true of the Episcopal or Anglican community (e.g., Cranmer, Ridley, Latimer, Hooper), the Lutheran churches (Luther himself), the Congregational churches (e.g., Owen, Goodwin, Ames, Cotton, Hooker), the Baptist churches (e.g., Roger Williams, and all five 'founders' of the Southern Baptist Convention), and above all, the Reformed and Presbyterian churches (e.g., Calvin, Beza, Knox). Even the Roman Catholics revere Augustine as the greatest of the church theologians, and on many of the matters with which we will be concerned, the 'Calvinists' were at one with him. Yet for all this consensus,

9

there is little understanding of the tradition or its practical importance. This is a source of frustration and regret for me, because I personally stand as one who has been profoundly touched by the practical implications of Calvinism, and deeply longs for others to drink from its satisfying wells. Yet in the popular mind, insofar as anything at all is understood about them, Calvinism's doctrines are regarded as irrelevant theological abstractions without any practical relevance at all.

What exactly will we be talking about? I won't try now to present the whole system of doctrine. For those wishing to review its contents, I refer you to the *Westminster Confession of Faith With Scripture Proofs*. For our purposes I will focus in on three cardinal doctrines, which shall serve as the focus for the first leg of our journey.

Our sovereign God

First, *the sovereignty of God*. If there is one doctrine for which Calvinism is known, it is this one. The Bible, say the Calvinists, teaches that God rules over all of creation, over all of history, decreeing and determining, in the words of the Shorter Catechism, 'whatsoever comes to pass.' Joseph can look back at his wretched circumstances when his brothers sold him into slavery and say 'God meant it for good' (Gen. 50:20). God says through Isaiah, 'I am... the One forming light *and* darkness, causing well-being *and* calamity, I am the Lord who does *all these*' (Isa. 45:7). He works '*all things* after the counsel of his will' (Eph. 1:11). He 'causes *all things* to work together for good' (Rom. 8:28). There are no exceptions to this. Sparrows don't fall out of trees and hairs don't fall out of heads apart from His will (Matt. 10:29, 30). Everything is controlled and determined by God. Including evil? In one sense yes, in another no. God is not the author of evil, but neither is evil running loose in God's universe outside of His sovereign purposes. Even the crucifixion, that most evil of all human deeds, was said by Peter at Pentecost to be carried out by the 'predetermined plan and foreknowledge of God' (Acts 2:23). The early church said that Herod and Pilate and the rest did whatever God's hand and purpose 'predestined to occur' (Acts 4:28).

Every atom of existence is under the direct control of God. There is not even 'one maverick molecule,' as R.C. Sproul says.[1] Everything is under the control of God.

Human depravity

The second cardinal doctrine is that of *the depravity of man.* Are people basically good or basically evil? The Christian church has historically said that people are by nature evil. Within Christendom, there is no theological perspective so pessimistic about human nature as that of Augustine and Calvin. Historically we have used the terminology of 'total depravity' to describe the human condition, meaning by it that people are corrupted, poisoned, and anti-God in all their faculties. Again, using the language of the Westminster Standards:

> (Man) is utterly indisposed, disabled, and made opposite unto all that is spiritually good, and wholly inclined to all evil and that continually (*Larger Catechism* Q. 25).

Is the Bible really as negative about humanity as this indicates? Survey the Scriptures. God said of man in the days of Noah that 'every intent of the thoughts of his heart was only evil continually' (Gen. 6:5). Through Jeremiah he says

---

1. R. C. Sproul, *Chosen by God*, Tyndale, p. 27.

of the human heart, 'The heart is more deceitful than all else and is desperately sick; who can understand it?' (Jer. 17:9). In Ecclesiastes we read, '... the hearts of the sons of men are full of evil, and insanity is in their hearts throughout their lives' (Ecc. 9:3). Paul, in Romans, quotes the Psalms in saying, 'as it is written, "there is none righteous, not even one; there is none who understands, there is none who seeks for God; all have turned aside, together the have become useless; there is none who does good, there is not even one" ' (Rom. 3:10-12). Jesus said simply, 'men loved the darkness rather than the light' (John 3:19,20). The problem is deep within us, in our desires, in our natures, in our loves and hates. Thus, we may summarize with Paul's ultimate metaphor, man is 'dead in his trespasses and sins' (Eph. 2:1-3). He is dead to good. He is dead to God. He is helpless, hopeless, and hellish.

Sovereign grace

Third, *the sovereignty of grace*. This follows necessarily from the previous two points. Man is so incapacitated by sin that unless God acts to rescue him nothing will happen. He will remain dead and blind. Thus the doctrine of the sovereignty of God, plus that of the depravity of man, leads us inexorably to the doctrine of *sovereign grace*. We cannot live spiritually unless we are born 'of God' or 'of the Spirit' (John 1:13; 3:8). We remain dead unless we are 'made alive' with Christ (Eph. 2:5). We cannot come to Him less He 'draws' us (John 6:44). We cannot choose Him unless He chooses us (John 15:16). We cannot love Him unless he first loves us (1 John 4:19). We cannot believe Him unless He gives us faith (Eph. 2:8,9). If we are to be saved God must sovereignly do it. 'By His doing you are in Christ Jesus,' Paul writes (1 Cor. 1:31). Salvation is 'of the Lord' (Jonah 2:9).

Who benefits from this sovereign and gracious intervention by God? Not all (or all would be saved), but some, specifically, those who are chosen. In the language of the *Westminster Confession of Faith*,

> By the decree of God, for the manifestation of his glory, some men and angels are predestinated unto everlasting life, and others fore-ordained to everlasting death. (III.3)

Calvin called this the *decretum horrible*. In the language of Scripture, 'He chose us in Him before the foundation of the world.... In love He predestined us' (Eph. 1:4,5). 'Well, that is just an isolated text,' you say. No, it would be truer to say that it is found on every page of Scripture. Work your way through the Book of Acts. Almost casually you will read that the number who believe is the same as the number whom 'the Lord shall call to Himself' (2:39); that God Himself 'adds' to the number of the church (2:47); that God Himself 'grants' repentance (5:31, 11:18); that the Lord 'opens' the heart (16:14); and most blatantly we read, 'as many as were ordained to eternal life believed' (13:48).

Turn to the Epistles. 'God has chosen you from the beginning for salvation,' Paul tells the Thessalonians (2 Thes. 2:13). He has 'saved us,' he tells Timothy,

> ... and called us with a holy calling, not according to our works, but according to His own purpose and grace which was granted us in Christ Jesus from all eternity (2 Tim. 1:9).

We could go on (and on!) but I think the point has been made. God is sovereign and grace is sovereignly dispensed.

If you're not convinced, we'll see overwhelming evidence in the pages ahead. Stay tuned.

Responses

Does this sound like 'good news' to you? For me, there is none better. Yet many react negatively. Let me summarize two such responses.

First, *those who aren't familiar with the Bible or sure that they believe it typically recoil in horror*. For them, the God described above is a monster. God, they would say, insofar as we know anything about Him, is kindly and good, but passively watching and remote. He doesn't control, and certainly doesn't predestinate anything. Moreover, for the unfamiliar and unbelieving, man is good. He may be misled by corruptions in his environment, but he is essentially benevolent. And man is paramount. Man's freedom, man's accomplishments, man's potentials are the name of the game for them, and both Calvinism's God and Calvinism's man assault their ambition for autonomous humanity.

Second, *even among Bible-believing Christians there is alarm*. This would especially be true of the many evangelical believers who are unaccustomed to thinking theologically. They don't *like* to think theologically. Their great question is 'what difference does it make?' If they can't see how it makes a difference in their lives they aren't interested. Now this is noteworthy because normally evangelical and fundamentalist types are fond of saying that they believe the whole Bible. But show them that 'predestination-stuff,' *right there in the Bible*, and they become strangely silent and uninterested. The discussion moves on.

In fact, when evangelical believers hear about the sovereignty of God, the depravity of man, and the sovereignty of grace, many are almost as horrified as the persons described above. They'll counter such talk with strong affirmations about 'free-will,' a term not found in the Bible, and 'whosoever will may come,' a phrase not found in the Bible. They may say, as I was told in the church of my youth, 'we don't know what it means, but it doesn't mean *that*.'

This would be even be true of many members of Presbyterian and Reformed churches. They may say that they believe their creeds and confessions and catechisms. But when this subject of election is brought up they, too, begin to grumble about 'what difference' it all makes, and how 'you'll get into heaven whether you understand that or not,' and how the important thing to do is to get on with the job of winning souls! All this theology is getting in the way of evangelism! We need to quit speculating and get on with preaching the gospel.

Does it make a difference? We are convinced that it does, and that it is vital that God's people understand the practical difference Calvinism makes. These doctrines are not just the theoretical musings of ivory-tower theologians. They are not just abstractions unconnected to life. They are central. They are vital. They are crucial to the living of life.

How so? Few seem to realize that these theological truths have shaped whole peoples and civilizations. Americans, of all people, ought to understand this. The nation was founded primarily by English Puritans, beginning at Plymouth Rock. Even though many other groups followed, their legacy was enduring. Among the other groups that did come to the American colonies, 85% of the population at the time of the American Revolution were of the Calvinistic heritage, being either English Puritans, Scotch-Irish Presbyterians, Dutch Reformed, German Reformed, or French Hugenot. What is their legacy? Such vital principles as the rule of law, due process, freedom of religion, democracy, limited government, free markets, a strong work ethic, stress upon education (Harvard was founded only a few years after the colony was established). All of these principles and points of emphasis flow directly from Calvinistic religion.[2] No wonder one German historian could call Calvin 'the virtual founder of America.'

Contemporary Christians ought also to understand it. The Calvinistic church has stood for representative government (in the electing of elders), for congregational participation in worship and congregational singing, for the centrality of the preached word, for the laity receiving communion in both kinds, for justification by faith alone, for the new birth and revivalCnot exactly a list of irrelevant items, many of which have been accepted even by Roman Catholics in their Vatican II reforms. Calvinism has played a vital role in giving both the modern world and the contemporary church their current shape.

But instead of looking at the institutional dimension (much as I would love to and may in the future), we will focus on the practical difference Calvinism makes in matters of personal piety, things such as assurance, humility, adversity, guidance, prayer, sanctification, and a thing we'll call 'outlook.' We will see the difference the doctrines of grace make right where we live and act and walk. Hopefully you'll never again to need to ask, 'what difference does it make?'

'My people perish for their lack of knowledge,' God warns through Hosea (Hos. 4:16). This surely has been our problem. We have not had the patience to wrestle with the

---

2. see Douglas Kelly, *The Emergence of Liberty in the Modern World*, P&R, 1992.

great truths. We have deliberately avoided certain doctrines. The result? The same result that occurs whenever one deliberately refuses any part of God's revelation of Himself. We suffer. We lose. Our souls don't receive the nourishment that that doctrine supplies. Our personalities are warped by that omission. Paul taught 'the whole counsel of God' because we need it all (Acts 20:27). If we didn't need a part of it, God would not have revealed it to us. Since He did, we can't go around saying, 'It's too hard,' or 'It's too theological.' Apply your minds. 'Come let us reason together,' the Lord says (Isa. 1:18).

This is what we intend to do in the pages ahead. I believe that the result will be a much expanded knowledge of God for most. With that will come a clearer understanding of life as well.

1

WORSHIP

Please read Romans 9:1–11:36; Ephesians 1:1-14

The goal of this book is practical divinity. What difference does it make if you believe the doctrines of man's total depravity and God's total sovereignty? Does it really make any impact upon one's life? Let me speak personally. The first great difference that these doctrines made in my life was that of transforming a self-centered, pew-sitting spectator into a worshiper of God. When I first wrestled with the high doctrines of God's sovereignty and man's depravity and reconciled myself to the Bible's teaching, I was overcome with awe. Up to that point, knowing God had been 'helpful' to me. I had grown considerably in spiritual maturity in college. But I hadn't really dealt with God except to treat Him as a personal asset. He was there for me. Of course, this is how so much of today's Bible teaching makes it seem. God is portrayed as the Ultimate Helper in dealing with self-image, anger, decision-making, fear, relationships, finances, etc. When I realized that He had saved me and that I was in His sovereign hand, it reordered my perspective. I came to realize both that He was far beyond the little boxes I had constructed for Him, and that I was there for Him, not Him for me. It made me bow in adoration before the God whom I was made to glorify.

Is my experience with the 'doctrines of grace' (another of our synonyms, heretofore called total depravity and total sovereignty) unusual? Not only is it not unusual, but I think that it takes on something approaching normative expectations

19

in the New Testament. The doctrine of predestination is not meant to be a point of theological disputation but a call to worship. This is exactly how Paul treats the subject in both Romans 9–11 and Ephesians 1, which we shall look at now in some detail.

The greatness of His power (Romans 9–11)
How is it that one explains that the people most familiar with the Scripture, who best knew the promises regarding the Messiah to come, missed Him when He came? This is a serious problem which Paul labors to explain in Romans 9– 11. Is the problem to be found in God Himself, or in God's gospel? No. 'It is not as though the word of God has failed,' he says. Then what is the answer? He continues, 'For they are not all Israel who are descended from Israel' (Rom. 9:6). Jewish unbelief is to be explained by the doctrine of election. God's sovereign choice is the ultimate reason why some believe and others do not. But don't think that this is a novel explanation. This is the way it has always been, from the beginning of redemptive (Bible) history, he tells them. Go back to Abraham. Wasn't he elect from among the nations? Why should he and his descendents be singled out as a 'chosen' people? Because God determined that it should be so. God sovereignly elected him.

Among Abraham's descendents, were they all saved? No. Ishmael was excluded: '... neither are they all children because they are Abraham's descendants, but: "Through Isaac your descendants will be named" ' (Rom. 9:7). Isaac was elect and Ishmael was not. Then move to the next generation. Isaac and Rebekah had twins, Jacob and Esau. What about them? '... for though the twins were not yet born, and had not done anything good or bad, in order that God's purpose according to His choice might stand, not because of works, but because of Him who calls, it was said to her, "The older will serve the younger." Just as it is written, "Jacob I loved, but Esau I hated" ' (Rom. 9:11-13). This is a particularly powerful illustration of the point because, by human standards, the two were as indistinguishable as two human beings can be – sharing the same mother and womb at the same time. Yet even before they were born, a choice was made by God. Thus, Abraham was elect and not anyone else, Isaac was elect and not Ishmael, and Jacob was elect and not Esau.

Paul will go on to show that even in his day there was a believing remnant among Israel through election: 'In the same way then, there has also come to be at the present time a remnant according to God's gracious choice' (Rom. 11:5). Israel was not rejected but still elect through the remnant. Through the elect remnant 'all Israel' would be saved (Rom. 11:26).

Is this fair? Interesting that you should ask. Paul anticipates your question. We read on: 'What shall we say then? There is no injustice with God, is there? May it never be!' (Rom. 9:14). But notice what his answer is: 'For He says to Moses, "I will have mercy on whom I have mercy, and I will have compassion on whom I have compassion." So then it does not depend on the man who wills or the man who runs, but on God who has mercy' (Rom. 9:15, 16). Paul doesn't explain how it is fair. He merely asserts God's right to do as he pleases. God answers to no one. If He wishes to show mercy He may. But He is not obligated to do so. Paul then points to the example of Pharaoh, whose heart God hardened and concludes: 'So then He has mercy on whom He desires, and He hardens whom He desires' (Rom. 9:18).

But it's not just, you say. How can He blame Pharaoh

when He hardened Pharaoh's heart? Again, Paul anticipates your complaint: 'You will say to me then, "Why does He still find fault? For who resists His will?" ' (Rom. 9:19)

What is the answer to that question? There isn't one. There is no denial that His will cannot be resisted. There is just a reminder that one is approaching impertinence. You have begun to challenge the ways of God and you don't know what you are talking about.

> On the contrary, who are you, O man, who answers back to God? The thing molded will not say to the molder, 'Why did you make me like this,' will it? Or does not the potter have a right over the clay, to make from the same lump one vessel for honorable use, and another for common use? What if God, although willing to demonstrate His wrath and to make His power known, endured with much patience vessels of wrath prepared for destruction? (Rom. 9:20-22)

These truths cannot be debated. They must be received. Paul is not asking you to understand, but submit. Your questions have gone too far, he says. Now you must sit down and be quiet. 'Who are you, O man?' he asks. Would you challenge God? By the way, the questions themselves prove that we have understood Paul accurately. There *is* the appearance of injustice! Yet justice is *not* explained; sovereignty is asserted.

Remarkably, Paul goes on in Romans 10 to clarify that the gate to heaven is closed to no one. How may one be saved? '... that if you confess with your mouth Jesus as Lord, and believe in your heart that God raised Him from the dead, you shall be saved' (Rom. 10:9). Again, 'For there is no distinction between Jew and Greek; for the same Lord is Lord of *all*, abounding in riches for *all* who call upon Him' (Rom. 10:12).

And again, 'for "*Whoever* will call upon the name of the Lord will be saved" ' (Rom. 10:13).

How do you explain how he can talk about election in one moment and then say 'whoever believes' will be saved? Now we've come to the point at which we have been driving. You don't explain it. Calvinists accept the apparent contradictions of God's sovereignty and human responsibility. We admit that we cannot reconcile these two principles. But we think that the Bible teaches both truths, so we teach both. If you try to reconcile one truth to the other you will compromise one or the other. 'Why reconcile friends?' Spurgeon asked.

What do we do with them? We bow in worship. This is exactly what Paul does. For three full chapters he pursues the subject. Finally, at the end of chapter 11 he can contain himself no longer, throws his hands up (as it were) at the mystery and cries out,

> Oh, the depth of the riches both of the wisdom and knowledge of God! How unsearchable are His judgments and unfathomable His ways! For who has known the mind of the Lord, or who became His counselor? Or who has first given to Him that it might be paid back to Him again? For from Him and through Him and to Him are all things. To Him be the glory forever. Amen (Rom. 11:33-36).

The sovereign, electing love of God leads Paul to praise God for His wisdom, His knowledge, and His incomprehensibility. This is a God who is bigger than Paul. He will not fit into any Paul-sized box. He reaches back to Isaiah for suitable language. 'Who has known the mind of the Lord?' No one has. No one has given Him counsel. Indeed, no one has given Him anything. For Paul, this is all to the greater praise of His glory.

This is the God 'from' whom are 'all things' and 'through' whom are 'all things' and 'to' whom are 'all things'. *All things* are *from* and *through* our God and *to* His glory.

This is what is so vital. We must all come to the place in our lives where we realize that we are dealing with One who is outside of our control. His will is not subject to ours. God sovereignly elects. He cannot be changed. He cannot be challenged. He cannot be manipulated. He cannot be controlled. This is a frightening thing. I am completely subject to the sovereign mercy of this God. I cannot argue with Him. I cannot bargain with Him. I cannot even understand Him. He transcends my logic. He exceeds all the categories of my experience and even my imagination. His ways are 'unfathomable'. I may be one of the great ones of the earth. I may have great power and authority in this world. When I bark orders, people may fall all over themselves trying to obey. I may always get what I want. I may always get my way. But with God this pattern comes to a screeching halt. He is in absolute control and I am helplessly at His mercy.

Do you know this God? I'm not asking if you know him intellectually or in theory. I am asking if you have looked into the face of the One who is Absolute Will and Absolute Power and felt your knees buckle? Nothing will cause you to bow in worship like the conviction that God is sovereign.

I say that this revelation is life-transforming because it will engender a new seriousness about life. Knowing that this is the God with whom I have to do, I'll be more careful about Sunday worship. I'll also be more serious about life generally, knowing that one day I will stand before such a God. Maybe before, I toyed with the things of God. No longer. Now I become much more careful to live in conformity with His commands.

The greatness of His grace (Ephesians 1, 2)

In the book of Ephesians we see the same outlook. Sinclair Ferguson makes a helpful comparison. Whereas in Romans 8 the doctrines of salvation are 'links in a chain' (predestination, calling, justification, glorification), in Ephesians 1 they are 'spokes in a wheel' which centres on Christ.[1] Chapter 1:3–3:21 is a continuous prayer of praise, the central theme of which is the electing love of God. 'He chose us in Him before the foundation of the world,' Paul says. 'He predestined us to adoption as sons,' he continues. The basis of this choice? 'According to the kind intention of His will, to the praise of the glory of His grace' (1:4-6). This is not a point of disputation. Paul is not writing in order to win an argument. He exults in the fact. Repeatedly, he speaks of God's will, intention, and purpose, saying even, 'we have obtained an inheritance, having been predestined according to His purpose who works all things after the counsel of His will,' and all 'to the praise of His glory' (1:11,12).

What does grace have to do with His choice? The Apostle Paul doesn't really explain. But there is a critical assumption that lies in the background of this whole discussion that must be understood for any of this to make sense. Not until 2:1 does he reveal it: 'And you were dead in your trespasses and sins' (Eph. 2:1).

Why is Paul so overwhelmed by the 'riches of His grace which He lavished on us' (1:7,8). Because he knows that it came to one who was spiritually 'dead'. The love which predestinates is a love which comes to a rebel. When God chooses or elects a person, it is a decision to love one who is lost in the mass of fallen, rebellious humanity. From a human race dead in sin, loving the darkness, hating God (Rom. 1:30-

---

1. Sinclair B. Ferguson, *Know Your Christian Life*, IVP, p. 20.

31), God decides to love and rescue some. He is obligated to save none. He decides to save some. He sent His Son to die for them, sent a preacher to explain the gospel, worked faith in their hearts, justified, adopted, sealed, and will one day glorify them. So Paul rejoices. He knows what he deserved – hell. What does he get? Heaven. 'In love He predestined us,' he says. It was love! 'He predestined us... according to the kind intention of His will.' He was kind! His grace is a praise-worthy grace and a glorious grace and a 'freely bestowed' grace (Eph. 1:6). Consider the 'riches of His grace,' such as was 'lavished upon us' (Eph. 1:7,8).

As we have seen, a true understanding of the sovereignty of God and the depravity of man leads us to appreciate not just God's greatness, but the greatness of His grace. Only when I truly understand the depth of my own depravity, my utter helplessness, and the sovereign, initiating love of God, can I understand the immensity of the grace of God. No other system of theology so abases man. No other says that man is so foul and helpless. No other, as a result, says that God has done so much to save us. The two go hand in hand. The greater man's need, the greater must be God's grace. When a child of God understands this, he is humbled. He bows. He who is forgiven much loves much (Luke 7:47). The Calvinist knows how much he has been forgiven. He asks with Isaac Watts, 'Alas and did my Saviour bleed and did my sovereign die? Would He devote that sacred head for *such a worm as I* ?' Listen to Calvinistic adoration:

> Was it for sins that I have done
> He groaned upon that tree?
> Amazing pity! Grace unknown!
> And love beyond degree!

And he responds,

> But drops of grief can ne'er repay
> the debt of love I owe;
> here, Lord, I give myself away;
> 'Tis all that I can do.

Where does a true comprehension of the doctrines of grace lead us? To our knees in worship. Perhaps one reason why so few are motivated to worship God with fervor is that we have reduced God to a slightly larger version of ourselves. He can be comprehended by our logic. He works within the bounds of our rules and reasons. He is so much like us that we see no real reason to worship Him. It is pathetic but true. What is the antidote? A God who is sovereign over the souls of wicked, undeserving sinners, including me.

This is the insight that was for me so life transforming. It inaugurated a Copernican revolution in my perspective—I realised I was displaced from the center of my universe and that God was enthroned there. It is a revolution which goes on.

What practical difference does Calvinism make? This first one is vital to all the rest. It will make you into a worshiper. When you come to realize that the God who is there is not subject to your desires, that He is sovereign over your eternity, and when you realize the greatness of His mercy and grace, you will begin to long for genuine worship, worship that prostrates you and exalts God.

Moreover, you will begin to experience a divinely given discontent with worship that is not worship. Entertainment that poses as worship will become distasteful to you. Revival meetings that pose as worship will leave your soul unsatisfied. Superficial song services, preaching services, and fellowship

services which fail to finally get around to worship will leave
the soul longing for worship that worships. Your soul will
crave and demand worship that is God-centered, that is filled
with high praise and lowly confession, and characterized by
a spirit of reverence and awe for the almighty Trinity. When
once you grasp the greatness of the sovereign God, your
worship will be transformed because *you* will be transformed,
hereafter to have the perspective of one who lives on his
knees.

2

HUMILITY

Please read 1 Corinthians 1:18-31

The third day of June, 1755, petition was made to King George II for a grant of land for the use by 'Dissenters from the Church of England and Professors of the Doctrines of the Church of Scotland, agreeable to the *Westminster Confession of Faith*'. Describing themselves as 'destitute of a House to meet in to worship according to the Form of their Confession', they petitioned to erect a 'Dissenting Meeting House'. George II granted their request, giving to the petitioners a public lot for the purpose of erecting 'a place of public worship for the service of Almighty God... for the use and benefit of such of our loving subjects now residing within the District of Savannah and are or shall be professors of the Doctrines of the Church of Scotland'.

We have been looking at the 'practical difference' the doctrines of the above mentioned Church of Scotland, those of the *Westminster Confession of Faith*, sometimes called 'Calvinism', sometimes called 'Reformed', sometimes called 'the doctrines of grace', make. Certainly one difference that they have made can be seen in the magnificent edifice that is the Independent Presbyterian Church of Savannah. Its building, plus the continuing health and vitality of this congregation, are testimonies to the power of the Reformed faith. Has Calvinism made a difference in matters of practical piety? Our answer has been a resounding yes.

Now we will look at humility.

Typically, history books will speak of the pride and arrogance engendered by the Calvinism of America's founding fathers. It is said that for them prosperity was a sign of election. The wealthy and successful looked at their material gain as proof that they were blessed by God and therefore among the 'chosen'. They looked with contempt at those who had less. The nation as a whole spoke of its 'manifest destiny' to rule the American continent. They after all were 'God's chosen people', and the Indians, Mexicans, or whoever else got in the way, were not. Thus Calvinism, so the argument goes, inevitably produces pride, arrogance, even criminal condescension.

I doubt if this interpretation of Calvinism's effects will stand up under scrutiny. Insofar as this describes Calvinism, it represents a secularization and corruption of it. Honest historians acknowledge this. I would go so far as to say that it represents the antithesis of the actual effects of Calvinism. If there is one certain effect of the Christian faith on character it is to produce humility. The classical world did not regard humility as a virtue. It saw it as weakness. Biblical religion regards it as a primary virtue, modeled by Moses and supremely seen in Christ (Num. 12:3; Matt. 11:29).

I'll take this a step further. A proud, condescending Christian, and especially a proud, condescending Calvinist, is a contradiction in terms. If one who has grasped the meaning of the doctrines of grace is proud, he is not a true Calvinist. He may have accepted a philosophy that resembles Calvinism. He may have been converted to a Reformed way of life, or a Reformed 'world and life view', but he is not a Calvinist. A true Calvinist is one who has been born again by the Spirit of God, who has seen his personal filth and corruption, who has fled to Christ, and knows better than anyone that it is only by the grace of God that he is saved. He has nothing to boast in. He has nothing to be proud about.

'But I know someone who is just like you describe,' someone objects, 'and he is Calvinistic and proud.' Admittedly something like this sometimes happens, and I think I know sometimes how. When one comes to understand the doctrines of the total depravity of man and the total sovereignty of God, it can be (as it was for me) like a second conversion. One's new understanding changes one's life. These doctrines become very dear to one, and one becomes very zealous to promote their dissemination. Converts to Calvinism will often look back with disdain on their former views, and when they hear others continuing to express them, they look with disdain upon them, and are quick to refute their every word. In their zeal, they quickly forget how recent their own 'conversion' has been, and how long they continued in error. They can appear to be arrogant and insensitive. They strike others as 'know-it-alls', and are unpleasant to be around. Understand this problem though we may, we still must say that this arrogance can only be a temporary aberration brought on by a 'convert's zeal'. Quickly he should return to the normal state of mind, which is profound humility. Here is why: the doctrine of election.

Your community (1 Corinthians 1:26-29)
Scan verses 1 Corinthians 1:26-29. Four times Paul repeats the words 'calling' or 'chosen'.

For consider your *calling*, brethren, that there were not many wise according to the flesh, not many mighty, not many noble; but God has *chosen* the foolish things of the world to shame the wise, and God has *chosen* the weak things of the world to shame the things which are strong, and the base things of the world and the despised, God has *chosen*, the things that are not, that He might nullify the things that are, that no man should boast before God.

What is Paul's point? He is dealing with a very proud Greek people. They were proud of their heritage. They were proud of their legacy of philosophy and worldly wisdom. Apparently there was an aristocratic element of sorts in the congregation who took pride in their lineage. So Paul reminds them of the truth about themselves.

First, the *message* that converted you is regarded by the world as a *foolish message*: 'For the word of the cross is to those who are perishing foolishness, but to us who are being saved it is the power of God' (1 Cor. 1:18). The great intellectuals are not touched by this message. They scoff at it. The scholars at the great universities of antiquity as well as modernity reject the gospel outright. So Paul asks them, 'Where is the wise man? Where is the scribe? Where is the debater of this age? Has not God made foolish the wisdom of the world?' (1 Cor. 1:20). The 'wise man', the 'scribe', the 'debater' all are on the other side. It would be nice if we had all the intellectuals agreeing with us, but we don't. Henry F. Schaeffer, Nobel Prize nominee in theoretical chemistry, told me that when he was at Berkeley there were not a half-dozen Christians on a faculty of several thousand. This is more typical than not. Where are the leading minds of our day? Are they professing Christians? If they do profess, do they live it? How many are zealous for Christ? 'The world through its wisdom *did not come to know God*,' Paul says (1:21). 'For indeed Jews ask for signs, and Greeks search for wisdom; but we preach Christ crucified, to Jews a stumbling block, and to Gentiles foolishness' (1 Cor. 1:22,23). No, our message is either an offense or foolishness. The great ones and the great mass utterly reject it.

Second, you have a *lowly preacher*. Listen to Paul's testimony about himself.

> And I was with you in weakness and in fear and in much trembling. And my message and my preaching were not in persuasive words of wisdom, but in demonstration of the Spirit and of power, that your faith should not rest on the wisdom of men, but on the power of God (1 Cor. 2:3-5).

There was nothing impressive about Paul. He was not an expert public speaker. He was speaking to a people who esteemed the arts of oration. This was their heritage. But here he came in 'weakness', in 'fear', and in 'much trembling'. He did not preach with 'persuasive words or wisdom'. Apparently he didn't have much in the way of style. Neither did he quote the famous philosophers or support his position with citations from contemporary thinkers. Why? Because he didn't want his converts to place their faith in the 'wisdom of men' but rather in 'the power of God' (2:5).

Commonly this has been the case. Jonathan Edwards was rejected by the intellectuals in Boston. The Wesleys and Whitefield were rejected by the learned authorities in the Church of England. Moody was rejected initially by everyone. Their style, their Biblicism, their lack of intellectual finesse, all led to rejection by the world. Your preachers are weak and lowly.

Third, your *fellow members* are lowly. Read again verses 26-29. 'Look at them,' Paul says, 'and learn the truth about yourselves.' From the human point of view, not many of your brethren are 'wise', 'mighty', or 'noble'. There may be some, but there are not many. The vast majority are what? They are 'foolish', 'weak', 'base', and 'despised'. They are 'the things that are not'. They are society's nobodies and rejects. They are not the elite. They are not people of quality. They are not from families of substance. Why? Because it is not God's design that they should be such. He chooses, chooses, chooses, Paul repeats three times, the weak and lowly so that he might 'shame' the great ones and 'nullify' their greatness. Through the weak he humbles the strong.

Sometimes we think, wouldn't it be great if so and so would join our church! Think what prestige he would bring to us. Think of what an asset he would be to the church. He's a blueblood! He's a professional! She's a success! In fairness it should be said that occasionally God does convert one of the great ones—the church has had its men and women of exceptional ability. The greatest man of late antiquity, without peer or rival, was Augustine. The greatest man of the Middle Ages was Aquinas. Calvin, Luther, Edwards, and Warfield were all men of consummate ability. But by and large this is the exception. Most believers are ordinary, humble, everyday people. God does not ordinarily choose the 'rich and famous'. He chooses the lowly. Does it sound like God is prejudiced against the great? No, remember we have said that the Bible does not compromise sovereignty at the expense of human responsibility or vice versa. There is a convergence of design between them. True, God does not choose them, but there is also typically an exceptional hardness of heart among the 'Great Ones'. They don't need God. They're doing just fine, thank you. They are quite pleased with themselves, and see no reason why God should not be so as well. And they don't want anyone, even God, telling them what to do. No one tells them what to do. No one is in authority over them. Pride is at the heart of the problem. Pride gets in the way. Pride won't admit need. Pride won't submit to Another. How many of the top corporate executives are Christians? How many of the famous Hollywood stars are Christians? How many of society's upper class are Christians? The church majority has always been simple people, humble enough to believe God and submit to him. As you look at the people around you in church, you have nothing to be proud of from a worldly point of view.

So look at your community. The simple *gospel* you believe is regarded as foolish. Your *leaders* are not esteemed by the world. Your *brethren* are lowly by the world's standards. Why? Because this has always been God's way. The Savior, after all, was not born in a palace but a stable. The disciples were not intellectuals but fishermen. There is nothing about the Christian community, as God has sovereignly constituted it, that can serve as a source of pride.

Your own conversion (1 Corinthians 1:29-31)

Well, maybe I can take pride in my own conversion, you think. After all, I went through a lengthy intellectual process. I weighed all the facts and then I made a decision. I decided that I would be a Christian.

Actually, that's not how it happened. Paul declares: 'But by His doing you are in Christ Jesus, who became to us wisdom from God, and righteousness and sanctification, and redemption' (1 Cor. 1:30). Then he quotes Jeremiah, 'that, just as it is written, 'LET HIM WHO BOASTS, BOAST IN THE LORD' (1 Cor. 1:31; Jer. 9:23, 24). Okay you made a decision. But you only made it because God made a decision first. Your decision is like the criminal who when led blindfolded to the edge of the cliff decided to cooperate with the authorities. Once he saw the situation he was in, there was no decision to be made. 'By His doing you are in Christ Jesus,' Paul says.

Oh, but I had the wisdom, you maintain. No, He 'became to us wisdom from God'. Any wisdom you possessed, God gave you.

Oh, but I had the faith, you counter. I trusted, I believed. No, faith is 'not of yourself,' but 'a gift of God' (Eph. 2:8). God gave you your faith.

Well, I did make a choice, you say. I chose Christ. By my own free will I decided. No, Jesus said, 'You did not choose Me, but I chose you' (John 15:16). Your choice was determined by His choice.

But there was love for God in my heart. I have always loved God. That's why I became a Christian. No, 'We love, because He first loved us' (1 John 4:19). Our love is a response to His love. There is *nothing* that you can boast about in any respect to your conversion.

Ah, but what about my growth as a Christian. I've really grown. I've learned so much. I've read the Puritans and all the books on marriage. And I know how to witness. Or perhaps your Christian life has a different focus. You have grown to have a burden for the needy. You give to the poor. You take into your home stray and lonely people. You are convinced that Christianity is more in the doing than in the theologizing. Hospitality and charity are hallmarks of your Christian discipleship. Can you be proud of your record? Can you look disdainfully on those who claim Christ but do none of these things? No, I'm afraid you can't take credit for any of this either. 'Christ,' says Paul, became to us our 'righteousness *and sanctification*'. Any measure of spiritual progress that you have made is God's work. The height of spiritual maturity to which you have attained is a gift from God. It is 'His doing'.

I believe that every Christian knows this, on his knees before God if at no other time. Paul says, 'by the grace of God I am what I am' (1 Cor. 15:10). The child of God knows this, especially if he understands the depths of human depravity as explained by the Reformed faith. He knows that he was dead in sin. He knows that he was deaf, blind, and uninterested. He knows that he was a 'lover of darkness' (John 3:19, 20). 'The natural man cannot understand the things of the Spirit of God,' Paul says (1 Cor. 2:14). He knows that it took a miracle of God to save him from his unbelief. It also took a miracle of God to save him from his ignorance and selfishness. He knows that 'salvation is of the Lord', and not of him (Jonah 2:9). If he is truly convinced of the truth of the doctrines of grace, there can be nothing of pride in him.

Everything else (1 Corinthians 4:7)
There are other potential sources of pride. One might take pride in one's physical beauty. Or one might take pride in one's worldly position. Or in one's accomplishments. One might think of oneself as a 'self-made man'. Paul is whittling down their pride in chapters 2 and 3, pride in worldly wisdom, and pride of party, and finally asks the bone-crunching question, 'For who regards you as superior? And what do you have that you did not receive? But if you did receive it, why do you boast as if you had not received it?' (1 Cor. 4:7).

There it is, Mr. Superiority. Let's evaluate your haughtiness. Let's take a look at your pride and arrogance. 'Who exactly is it that regards you as superior?' Is it the people of God? Is it God Himself? Does anyone else's opinion matter, when you come right down to it? Of course not. On the great day of Judgment, only God's opinion will matter. And *He* does not regard you as superior. Then who does? The world? On the basis of the values of the world you are a somebody? What a mist! What a fleeting, vanishing nothing! Have you been living for the opinion of the unregenerate, disappearing world?

Now let's look at your accomplishments more closely. So you have done great things. Who made you? Who gave to you the natural abilities that you have? Who gave your skills and intelligence? Then look at your opportunities. We Calvinists believe that God has decreed every moment of every day of our lives. Every open door, every experience, every opportunity has been given to us from Him. Just for the sake of clarification, let's consider what you might have amounted to if you had been born in the middle of an obscure country. The fact is, no matter how prestigious your bloodlines are, no matter how clever you are, no matter how hard working you are, you could be living today in primitive circumstances. 'What do you have that you didn't receive?' Then how can you boast? Everything that you have and are, morally, socially, vocationally, and religiously is a gift from him.

I have been amazed to find non-Christians using the phrase, 'There but for the grace of God....' Do you know the origins of that expression? It goes back to the English Reformer John Bradford. He was walking down the street and passed a drunk lying in the gutter. While others showed contempt for the 'bum', Bradford, a Calvinist said, 'There but for the grace of God lies John Bradford.' He understood the implications of the doctrines of grace. God has made us what we are. We can glory in nothing. 'By the grace of God I am what I am' (1 Cor. 15:10). How then can I too harshly judge another? But for the grace of God, I commit their sin. But for the grace of God I copy their failure.

Is this your outlook? The most humble people in the world ought to be those who believe the doctrines of grace. They, better than anyone, know that only by the grace of God do we amount to anything in this world, and escape hell in the next.

3

ADVERSITY

Please read Romans 8:26-39; Genesis 50:15-21

In 1858, a gifted young Presbyterian missionary named John G. Paton sailed with his wife and infant son to the New Hebrides in the South Pacific to begin missionary work among the islanders. Within a few months of his arrival, both his infant son and his wife had died, leaving him to labor alone.

In August of 1876, a gifted young theologian named Benjamin Breckinridge Warfield and his bride were honeymooning in Germany. While sightseeing in the Black Forest region, they were suddenly caught in a severe storm, and something that was never quite explained happened to his bride, rendering her an invalid for the rest of their lives together.

In the 1950s the Independent Presbyterian Church of Savannah congregation called a young preacher to take the reins of a very divided church. He came with his wife and their five children, the youngest only three years old. Within a year and a half, Anton Van Puffelen developed a brain tumor, and in just over two years after he started his work in Savannah the Rev. Van Puffelen was dead.

How do you explain these things? Perhaps just as baffling, how do you explain the responses of these individuals? John G. Paton stayed on the field and reaped a great harvest, later saying:

I built the grave round and round with coral blocks, and covered the top with beautiful white coral, broken small gravel; and that spot became my sacred and much-frequented shrine, during all the following months and years when I laboured on for the salvation of these savage Islanders amidst difficulties, dangers and deaths. Whensoever Tanna turns to the Lord, and is won for Christ, men in after-days will find the memory of that spot still green—where with ceaseless prayers and tears I claimed that land for God in which I had 'buried my dead' with faith and hope.[1]

Warfield cared for his wife the remaining forty years of their adult life together, humbly, submissively, without complaint, without self-pity, without justifying a need for his own fulfilment, fulfilling his marital vows, doing his duty toward his wife.

'Mrs. Van,' as she was known in Savannah, gentle and meek on the surface, tough as nails underneath, began to teach in the Independent Presbyterian Day School and reared her five children at tremendous self-sacrifice, again without complaint.

What was the key in each of these situations? The key is that each believed in the sovereignty of God. Each understood God's justice, His mercy, His absolute rule, and each received their circumstances as from His hand for their good and submitted to it.

Still, how do you explain adversity? How do you deal with the suffering that is in the world? Granted that it takes time for our emotions to catch up with our minds, that there are no 'easy' answers, and that when we answer the 'why' question

---

1. Iain Murray, *The Puritan Hope*, Banner of Truth, pp. 179,180.

we must do so not simplistically or matter of factly; yet we do have an explanation for suffering, the only explanation for suffering that works and makes room for comfort in a world of pain.

The problem of pleasure

From our point of view, much of the discussion of 'the problem of pain' and suffering gets started on the wrong foot. As we saw in our consideration of predestination, there is a tendency to begin with the assumption of human innocence. Adversity then is viewed as an unfair or unjust intrusion into the life of one who is undeserving. This is implicit in almost all of the popular discussions of the subject. Thus we regularly question, 'Why would God have allowed this to happen to such a fine (and undeserving) family?'

The Biblical place to begin any consideration of suffering is not with innocence but guilt. At the beginning of the Bible is an account of what is called the 'Fall of Man'. It is there to remind us that we live in a 'fallen' world, a world in disarray and under God's curse. The response of God to the sin of Adam and the sins of his progeny is judgment. God promised death 'in the day that you shall eat of it'. Death, in a final sense, however, was postponed. In the meantime, life consists of multiple mini-judgments which are visited upon us because of the sin of Adam and our own sins, as previews of the final judgment. These mini-judgments, because they fall short of eternal death in hell, are, in effect, gracious stays of execution.

What we are saying is that each moment that each of us exists on this side of hell is a problem. How is it that a just and true God can tolerate evil and let it go on existing? How can he delay his warning that 'the soul that sins, it shall die' (Ezek. 18:4)? The problem is not a problem of pain but of pleasure.

Strict justice lands each of us in hell. Anything less than that—
sickness, injury, poverty, hunger, or heartbreak—is mercy.

Consider Jesus' answer to the disciples' question about
the hapless Galileans who had been butchered by Pilate
(Luke   13). They wanted to know if 'these Galileans were
greater sinners than all other Galileans because they suffered
this fate'. The question is an old one. Do those who suffer
suffer because they are more sinful than other people? Can
we say that suffering is directly proportionate to sin? The
popular answer is to say, 'No,' and this answer is correct. We
can accurately cite Job as an example of a man who was not
suffering for his personal sin. Jesus, indeed, says, 'I tell you,
no....' Jesus agrees with the popular answer in saying that
these folks were not necessarily more deserving of suffering
than others. They did not die because they were greater
sinners than the rest. We expect Him to go on as we might and
talk about how the undeserving suffer. Many times, we
would say, the innocent are made to suffer in the world.
Often, we say, it is the good who are injured and hurt. But,
surprise, this is *not* what He says at all. Instead of saying that
some are innocent sufferers, he says that *everyone* deserves
to suffer in this way. He warns that 'unless you repent, you
will *all likewise perish*'. In other words, it is not that they
were worse than others, but this is what every sinner deserves
and will get unless he repents. Jesus focuses not on the
tragedy that has befallen the few, but on the grace by which
the majority are spared.

Similarly, Jesus went on to speak of the eighteen on whom
the 'tower of Siloam fell and killed'. He asks, 'were (they)
worse culprits than all the men who live in Jerusalem?' Can
we deduce, from the amount of suffering people endure, who
is righteous and who is sinful? No, he says. But again, does

this mean that they might be undeserving? No. They got what everyone deserves but some are spared.

> I tell you, no, but unless you repent, you will all likewise perish (Luke 13:5).

Thus, the problem of suffering as Jesus interprets it is not a problem of pain at all. Pain can be explained easily. We live in a fallen world that is under judgment. All of life's picnics have ants. On our honeymoon, Emily and I set aside a day for the beach. About the time we arrived, it started to rain. Not being the theologian of the family, she asked, 'Why would God do this to us?' My sensitive response was, 'Why hasn't it rained everyday? Why did He allow us to come here at all?' She was not amused. Of course, there is suffering. The remarkable thing is not that there is pain but that there is pleasure. Once one understands the doctrine of the Fall and of the depravity of man the philosophical problem is not that of explaining why God allows suffering but why He shows mercy and grace. Any pain and suffering less than the flames of eternal fire in hell is a merciful reprieve from God. I can understand why we suffer. I can't understand why we don't suffer more.

Sovereignty and pain
In previous chapters we have seen that the sovereignty of God extends over every molecule of existence. He has decreed and planned 'whatsoever comes to pass'. Don't, then, think for a moment that your pain is excluded. When I was in seminary, a very promising young Christian, a Cal Tech student gifted with a brilliant mind, was heading for the mission field with Wycliffe Bible Translators. He fell on a hiking trip and was tragically killed. A world famous

evangelical theologian said at his funeral, 'This was not the will of God.' At a funeral in Savannah a few years ago, a similar statement was made of the unexpected death of a relatively young mother: 'God did not want this to happen.' This is also the position taken in the very popular book *Why Bad Things Happen to Good People*. The author lost his teenage daughter to leukaemia. He wrestled with explaining how God could have allowed it to happen. Notice his frame of reference. There are 'good' (read 'innocent') people who don't deserve to have 'bad' things happen to them. The answer that he settled on was that God is good, but there is nothing that He can do about suffering. He can't interfere. His hands are tied. He is not at fault. He is not to be blamed. We can be sure that He still loves us because He is not the one who did this awful thing to us.

What can we say to this? In our view, this explanation offers no consolation whatsoever and, indeed, is horrifying. Why? Consider the following:

First, if there is a God, *what happens must be His will*. If anything happens that is not His will, He is not God, and we are in trouble. If there are stray molecules wandering around doing things that He has not ordained, then God has a competitor out there equal to Himself, and He is not God as the Bible describes Him. For God to be God He must be sovereign. For Him to be sovereign *at all* He must be sovereign *of all*.

Let me see if I can clarify what I mean. All who believe in God believe that God foresees all things. Once you give up believing in foreknowledge, you've really stopped believing in God. What He foreknows is certain to happen. So when God foreknows a thing and decides to allow it to happen, he does so because it suits His purposes. It fits His plan. The alternative is to say that He foresees things and allows them even though they don't suit His purposes, which is clearly illogical and silly. It doesn't mean He 'likes' what He foresees, just that He allows it to happen because He finds some positive purpose in it and reason for it. The good God permits to happen what He permits to happen because it suits His purposes; and His purposes are good.

Sometimes people try to evade the implications of this by appealing to foreknowledge, saying that God merely 'foresees' all things, He doesn't actually will them. But as we can see, this distinction won't hold up. What an omnipotent God foreknows and permits, He wills and ordains.

Second, *events either have God-given meaning or they have no meaning at all.* In an attempt to get God 'off the hook', people end up emptying their tragedies of meaning, so rendering them truly tragic. It needs to be recognized that you can't have it both ways. Either God is in it, or He isn't. If He isn't, then it is just the devil, bad 'luck', fate, or chance.

When I was the youth minister in Miami we experienced two tragic deaths of fathers with young teenagers. One was my wife Emily's father who suffered a heart attack when she was just sixteen. The other was also a sixteen-year-old girl, but the circumstances were different. Whereas Emily's father died suddenly, this man, the Rev. J.R. Richardson's son, Dr. John Richardson, died very gradually over a period of nearly two years. The final days were unlike anything I had seen before or have seen since. He died at home surrounded by his family. His last moments were spent with his youngest daughter snuggled up next to him on one side, another daughter at his feet, his wife on the other side, his sons seated beside the bed. It was the saddest and the sweetest death I had ever seen. A few weeks later, that youngest daughter came to

me and asked, 'Why would God allow this?' My answer was
to gently say, 'Oh, but He did, and He has *good* reasons,' and
then to go on and say, 'and we cling to this because the only
alternative is to say that God didn't allow this and there are
no reasons and it is just a tragedy devoid of any purpose.'
Now what must you do? Trust Him! Say God isn't responsible,
and you remove the opportunity to trust Him.

'God is great and God is good.' That was the first prayer
that I learned. It also expresses the problem of suffering. Why
does a *great* God allow evil when He could stop it? Why does
a *good* God allow evil when He hates it? Deny either side of
the equation and you solve the problem of evil. God is good
but not great; He would like to prevent evil, but he is weak.
God is great but not good; he doesn't want to prevent evil
because He delights in it.

Since Augustine (remember we are 'Augustinians'),
Christians have been saying that God permits evil for the
greater good. The paradigm is found in the crucifixion. When
man did the greatest evil, God brought from it the greatest
good. But the crucifixion was carried out by the 'predetermined
plan and foreknowledge of God' (Acts 2:23). God was in it;
He had ordained it. Likewise, He is in our suffering. Because
He is in it, it has a purpose, it has meaning.

Christ and pain
Finally, we come to the answers found in Romans 8. The
wonder of our adoption and eventual glorification lead Paul
to speak of the path to glory which is the path of *suffering*. We
are 'fellow-heirs with Christ,' he says, 'if indeed we suffer
with Him in order that we may also be glorified with Him'
(8:17). Again, he joins suffering and glory saying, 'For I
consider that the sufferings of this present time are not worthy

to be compared with the glory that is to be revealed to us' (Rom. 8:18). He speaks of our 'groaning' and contrasts it with 'our adoption as sons, the redemption of our body' (8:23). He urges the need of 'hope' and 'perseverance' (8:24, 25). He promises the help of the Spirit when we pray 'with groanings too deep for words' (v. 26). Then comes the crown jewel of Bible promises: 'And we know that God causes all things to work together for good to those who love God, to those who are called according to His purpose' (Rom. 8:28). Paul exults in a God who is in all things causing all things to work for the good of those who love Him. And just in case you might pause and doubt if you love God sufficiently, he adds, 'to those who are called according to His purpose.' Machen said of these verses:

> ... how little comfort there would be in those words if the verse stopped there—if we had been told merely that all things work together for good to them that love God, and then we had been left to kindle that love of God in our cold, dead hearts. But, thank God, the verse does *not* end there. The verse does not just say: 'All things work together for good to them that love God.' No, it says: 'All things work together for good to them that love God, to them who are the called according to His purpose.' There, my friends, is the true ground of all our comfort—not in our love, not in our faith, not in anything that is in us, but in that mysterious and eternal counsel of God from which comes all faith, all love, all that we have and are and can be in this world and in the world to come.[2]

---

2. J. Gresham Machen, *The Christian View of Man*, Banner of Truth, p. 68.

The ones who love God are the ones who are called. The called are those who are foreknown (which means fore-loved) and predestined. The 'golden chain' is laid out in verse 30: 'and whom He predestined, these He also called; and whom He called, these He also justified; and whom He justified, these He also glorified' (Rom. 8:30). Those whom God has set His love upon – who have been called to Christ effectually by the gospel, who are justified and glorified (the past tense indicates that Paul sees even this as an accomplished fact) – these are promised that everything has a good purpose for them. God Himself guarantees it.

When I was three, my parents absent-mindedly left my sister and me in the family station wagon when we got home from church one Sunday afternoon. We played. I released the emergency brake. The car began to roll down the driveway. We panicked. My sister jumped out. She was five—she could do that. I fell out and under the front wheel, and our '56 Plymouth station wagon rolled up my back and neck and over my head.

When I was fifteen, I was practising with the varsity football team that included three future college all-Americans, including Vince Feragammo. One afternoon I ran a 'quick-out' pattern, caught the ball, turned up field, tried to evade my defender, and in the midst of evading him, suddenly felt a sharp pain in my thigh. All over the field a loud noise like a tree-branch cracking could be heard as I fell, my leg twisted under me, my femur freakishly broken.

Why? I don't know. I don't have to know. All I have to know is that God was in it, and He was working it for good.

Some of you have suffered far worse than this. Some of you have lost children and grandchildren to accidents and diseases. Others have been devastated through the deaths of husbands and wives. Friends, relatives, other loved ones have suffered from tragic circumstances. You have cried out, 'Oh no, not this—anything but this! Lord, why? Why would you do this?' Perhaps you have grown bitter. You have resented God ever since. You're disillusioned and confused. Know this for certain—in Christ, though the devil, the world, and your enemies have meant your destruction, God was working all things for good.

Consider the life of Joseph. What adversity he suffered! Think of the heartbreak of total rejection by his own brothers who were ready to kill him on the spot. Think of the grief of being sold into slavery, of forcibly leaving his family and not seeing them again for decades. Even in Egypt he had to deal with a false accusation of rape by Potiphar's wife which landed him in jail. There was in his life plenty of opportunity for bitterness. Think of all that God had allowed to happen. Robbed of his childhood, robbed of his homeland and family, robbed of his good name, why should he not curse God? But what does he say? He sees the sovereign hand of God in it all. First, he tells his brothers, 'Now, therefore, it was not you who sent me here, but God; and He has made me a father to Pharaoh and lord of all his household and ruler over all the land of Egypt' (Gen. 45:8). And a second time he says, 'And as for you, you meant evil against me, but God meant it for good in order to bring about this present result, to preserve many people alive' (Gen. 50:20). Read it again. 'God meant it for good,' he says.

Many times, even most times, we won't know what good God is bringing from adversity. That is not the critical thing. The critical thing is knowing that God is good and He meant it! When you lost your loved one, He meant it. When you were afflicted with disease, God meant it. When you were hit with financial reversals, God meant it. He promises to bring good from it. Now you must trust Him.

Do the high Calvinistic doctrines really make a difference? Does belief in the sovereignty of God make any practical impact upon life? I hope that you are beginning to see that these doctrines are vital. Only when we understand that God has ordained our suffering can we begin to make sense of it. Only then can we be certain that He has a purpose in it. When tragedy comes, when adversity strikes, we will not be shaken. Yes, we will cry. Yes, we will grieve. But we will move on confidently knowing that God is on His throne, that we are in His hand, that our circumstances are His doing, and He is working them for our good.

4

OUTLOOK

Please read Job 1:5-22; 2 Corinthians 12:1-10

Read the following account of suffering found in Ben Haden's famous sermon entitled 'Affliction':

The late Dr. Donald Barnhouse told how once he was conducting a week of services in a large church. The pastor of that church was on the 'hot seat.' His wife was about to have their first child. This was a source of great anxiety for the pastor, but it was a source of real humor for Dr. Barnhouse and he joked about it throughout the week.

On his last night, when he went to the podium, Dr. Barnhouse waited and waited for the pastor to introduce him. But the pastor didn't come. So smiling, and in a knowing fashion, Dr. Barnhouse got up, introduced himself, and conducted the service that night.

Toward the end of that service Dr. Barnhouse noticed the pastor as he slipped in at the back of the sanctuary and made his way silently to the podium. When the pastor took his seat Dr. Barnhouse turned and smiled at him in a knowing fashion. All the congregation joined him in smiling. Then Dr. Barnhouse continued the service and completed it.

It was at this point that Dr. Barnhouse asked the young pastor, 'Everything all right?' No one had noticed the pastor's expression.

'Could I see you in my study, Sir?' the pastor asked Dr. Barnhouse.

'Certainly,' Dr. Barnhouse said,

So they made their way to the pastor's study. Then the pastor blurted out, 'Dr. Barnhouse, our child is a *mongoloid.* I haven't told my wife, and I don't know what I'm going to tell her.'

'My friend, this is *of the Lord,*' Dr. Barnhouse said. And he turned to this passage, the most overlooked passage in all the Old Testament, the fourth chapter of Exodus, and he read aloud:

And the Lord said unto him, who hath made man's mouth or who maketh the dumb or deaf or the seeing or the blind... hath not I—the Lord?

'Let me see that,' the pastor said. And he studied it very quietly. As he studied it, Dr. Barnhouse said, 'My friend, you know in the promise in Romans 8 that all things, *including this mongoloid child,* work together for good to those that love the Lord.'

The pastor closed the Bible. He left the study and he went straight to the hospital room of his wife. As he walked in, she was saying, 'Cap, I want to see my baby. I've asked to see my baby and they won't let me. Is anything wrong with my baby?'

Who maketh the dumb, dumb and the blind, blind and the deaf, deaf... is it not I, the Lord? 'My precious darling, the Lord has blessed us with a mongoloid child.'

The young wife and mother cried long and hard. Then she said, 'Where did you get *that*?'

'From God's own Word.'

'Let me see it.' And then she read it...

When that pastor's wife called her mother she (said), 'Mother, the Lord has blessed us with a mongoloid child. We don't know the nature of the blessing but we do know it's a blessing.'

There were no tears, no hysteria, no breakdown, no coming apart at the seams . . .

The following Sunday the pastor was back in his pulpit. In the congregation, unknown to him, were the telephone operator and seventy nurses from that hospital.

At the conclusion of that service, as he always did, the pastor stood down front and he said, 'If you've never met Jesus Christ I want to extend to you the invitation to come down to the altar and to receive him as your personal Lord and your personal Saviour.'

The pastor barely glanced up because this was his custom since very few ever came. Thirty nurses from the hospital came to the altar that day!

Can you imagine one mongoloid child being patently responsible for giving eternal life to thirty nurses? You say, 'How horrible!' No, my friend, not horrible.

Does this story sound impossible to you? Well, it is possible. In fact, we have personally known a young couple in our church whose infant son has Down's Syndrome who found deep consolation in Romans 8:28 and Psalm 139 and the certainty that their child was not an accident but was fashioned in the womb by God Himself and given to them to rear. As they have put it, though shocked at first by the news of his condition, they now *would have it no other way!*

Let me sum up what we have said about adversity. Wherever you find yourself, whatever your circumstances, whatever you encounter, you are *always* dealing with God. He is inescapable. Even the damned in hell are dealing with God. The Psalmist says, 'If I make my bed in Sheol, behold, Thou art there' (Ps. 139:8). At every point in life I encounter God and I can and must respond appropriately.

This perspective is life-transforming. Those who are certain that what happens happens by the hand of God look at life differently than those who don't. They have a distinctive outlook. The conviction that 'God is the author of my circumstances' enables the believer to live life with unparalleled peace and joy, for the reasons we shall see below.

Sovereignty and gratitude

Paul explains in his second Epistle to the Corinthians that he had been privy to extraordinary revelations. He was caught up to the 'third heaven', to 'Paradise' (12:2). Because he might have been tempted to become proud about these unique experiences, he was given special afflictions designed to keep him humble.

And because of the surpassing greatness of the revelations, for this reason, to keep me from exalting myself, there was

given me a thorn in the flesh, a messenger of Satan to
buffet me—to keep me from exalting myself! (2 Cor.
12:7)

Notice how he speaks of it. On the one hand, he sees the
purposes of God in it. The affliction was given 'to keep me
from exalting myself.' On the other hand, he calls it 'a
messenger of Satan.' Which was it? Who was behind it? God
or Satan? The answer is both. Satan was the agent of affliction
who undoubtedly was carrying out his own wicked designs.
But the afflicting itself was the will of God. Satan, in trying
to destroy Paul was, in effect, serving the purposes of God.
Paul begs to be relieved of the affliction (whatever it was—
we don't know): 'Concerning this I entreated the Lord three
times that it might depart from me' (2 Cor. 12:8). Yet he
receives this answer: 'And He has said to me, "My grace is
sufficient for you, for power is perfected in weakness" (2 Cor.
12:9a). Paul's response? He rejoices! 'Most gladly, therefore,
I will rather boast about my weaknesses, that the power of
Christ may dwell in me' (2 Cor. 12:9b).

Why is Paul glad? Because he sees the good purposes of
God in it. Then why does he blame Satan? Because if there
had been no Fall, there would be no suffering. If the human
race were not in rebellion against God and if the human heart
were not 'deceitful above all else and desperately wicked,'
then pain and sorrow would be unknown in this world. When
suffering comes, it is valid to become angry with the immediate
causes of evil. Grieve for the fallen state of the world. Let
righteous indignation rise in your heart against the devil and
wicked men. Call it a 'messenger of Satan.' He is at fault for
the pain we endure. In your prayers, long for the day of his
destruction. But remember, that behind it all are the purposes

of God who permits and ordains these things for our good. It is a messenger of Satan, *but* it fulfills the purposes of God. It was Satan who afflicted Job. But he saw behind Satan the plan of God. When told of the destruction of his wealth and the death of his children, his response was dramatic and exemplary:

> Then Job arose and tore his robe and shaved his head, and he fell to the ground and worshiped. And he said, 'Naked I came from my mother's womb, and naked I shall return there. The LORD gave and the LORD has taken away. Blessed be the name of the LORD.' (Job 1:20-21)

Was it the devil? Yes. Is the devil God's devil, fulfilling His purposes in spite of himself? Yes. Are we not at all points dealing with God? Yes. 'The Lord gave and the Lord has taken away.' Can we not bless God and give thanks then? Yes! Yes!

Paul says, 'Rejoice always... In everything give thanks' (I Thess. 5:16-18). How can one do that? By seeing the good purposes of a good God in everything. Paul could see that God's power was being 'perfected in weakness'. There is positive value in pain!

> 'For those whom the Lord loves He disciplines, and He scourges every son whom He receives.' It is for discipline that you endure; God deals with you as with sons; for what son is there whom his father does not discipline? But if you are without discipline, of which all have become partakers, then you are illegitimate children and not sons. Furthermore, we had earthly fathers to discipline us, and we respected them; shall we not much rather be subject to

the Father of spirits, and live? For they disciplined us for a short time as seemed best to them, but He disciplines us for our good, that we may share His holiness. All discipline for the moment seems not to be joyful, but sorrowful; yet to those who have been trained by it, afterwards it yields the peaceful fruit of righteousness (Heb. 12:6-11).

Look carefully at those statements. Affliction is the means by which God disciplines us. This discipline is 'for our good.' Why? 'That we may share His holiness.' While temporarily 'sorrowful,' yet we are 'trained' by it, and 'afterwards it yields the peaceful fruit of righteousness.' These prepare us for service and for heaven!

Affliction is our gymnasium. Athletes do not improve their skills except through painful training. It is the same for the kingdom. In fact, you may be interested to know that the slogan, 'No pain, no gain,' found in gyms throughout the country may be found in Charles Hodge's *Systematic Theology*, published in the 1870s. It is only 'Through many tribulations we must enter the kingdom of God' (Acts 14:22). James says,

Consider it all joy, my brethren, when you encounter various trials, knowing that the testing of your faith produces endurance. And let endurance have its perfect result, that you may be perfect and complete, lacking in nothing (Jas. 1:2-4).

Peter writes,

In this you greatly rejoice, even though now for a little while, if necessary, you have been distressed by various trials, that the proof of your faith, being more precious than gold which is perishable, even though tested by fire, may be found to result in praise and glory and honor at the revelation of Jesus Christ;.... (1 Pet. 1: 6-7)

Paul says,

And not only this, but we also exult in our tribulations, knowing that tribulation brings about perseverance; and perseverance, proven character; and proven character, hope; and hope does not disappoint, because the love of God has been poured out within our hearts through the Holy Spirit who was given to us. For while we were still helpless, at the right time Christ died for the ungodly. (Rom. 5:3-6)

They speak of 'trials', 'temptations', 'testing', and 'tribulations'. Yet, in each case, the apostles see positive value in suffering. God is in it working His good purposes for us. Therefore, 'consider it all joy', 'greatly rejoice', 'exult', because you and your faith are being tested and proved.

Peter and John were beaten and threatened by the authorities. Their response?

So they went on their way from the presence of the Council, rejoicing that they had been considered worthy to suffer shame for His name. (Acts 5:41)

This is remarkable, isn't it? They are grateful! They rejoice! They see the value in it! They see the privilege in it! They see God in it!

Malcolm Muggeridge said it well:

As an old man... looking back on one's life, it's one of the
things that strikes you most forcibly—that the only thing
that's taught one anything is suffering. Not success, not
happiness, not anything like that. The only thing that really
teaches one what life's about...is suffering, affliction.'[1]

You can be grateful in every circumstance in life because
your circumstances are the means God uses to save your soul.
How many would believe if they had not suffered? For some,
a marriage had to fall apart. Some had to lose a loved one.
Some had to see their business collapse. Some had to be fired
from a job. Others, who were already believers, have only
grown in proportion to their suffering. Pain, and only pain,
has led to self-examination, to acknowledgment and
confession of sin, to humble dependence upon God. Pain, and
only pain, has driven you to your knees, has caused you to
hunger and thirst for God and His righteousness, has caused
you to search the Scriptures for truth. Only in the context of
suffering have you grown. God's 'power is perfected in
weakness,' Paul says to us. He draws the ironic conclusion,
'for when I am weak then I am strong' (2 Cor. 12:9,10).
Rejoice and give thanks for your afflictions! This is the outlook of one who sees all his circumstances as ordered by God.

2. Sovereignty and contentment
Look again at what the Apostle Paul says.

Therefore I am well content with weaknesses, with insults,
with distresses, with persecutions, with difficulties, for
Christ's sake; for when I am weak, then I am strong. (2
Cor. 12:10)

---

1. *National Review*, December 17, 1990, p. 62.

He says, 'I am well content....' It is amazing, isn't it? He is content with 'weaknesses, with insults, with distresses, with persecutions, with difficulties.' Why? Because they are 'for Christ's sake.' Christ is in them. These afflictions are not just the devil running wild. Don't attribute your pains merely to the actions of wicked men. God is behind them. Your suffering is fulfilling His purposes. Knowing this, we can be content. If this is what our sovereign Lord wants, then I can live with it, even thrive in it.

Look at Paul describe his outlook in his Epistle to the Philippians:

> Not that I speak from want; for I have learned to be content in whatever circumstances I am. I know how to get along with humble means, and I also know how to live in prosperity; in any and every circumstance I have learned the secret of being filled and going hungry, both of having abundance and suffering need (Phil. 4:11-12).

The Philippians were being complimented by Paul for coming to his assistance in time of need. But he wants them to know that even in deprivation he was content. Even if they had not come to his assistance, he would still have been content. 'I have learned,' he says, 'to be content in whatever circumstances I am.' With 'humble means,' he is content. When 'going hungry,' he is content. If 'suffering need,' he is content. We notice that he is content with 'prosperity,' when 'filled,' and 'having abundance,' but this doesn't surprise us. What is surprising is that he is content 'in any and every circumstance.' How does he do it?

> I can do all things through Him who strengthens me (Phil. 4:13).

Christ is in it. It is His will for Paul to be in the circumstances
he is in. So He strengthens him for the tasks to which he is called.

If you believe Christ is sovereign, that He has called you into
the circumstances you encounter, then you should be content.
Often, however, this seems not to be the case. Why are so many
Christians not content these days? I can think of two reasons.

First, some of them fail to believe the very thing we are
talking about. They don't believe God is in their circumstances.
So, when they encounter poverty, they become enormously
unhappy. They look around at what others have and they
think, 'Why can't I have nice things? Why can't I have a new
car? Why can't I buy beautiful clothes?' They can see nothing
redeeming about their poverty. Instead, they envy those who
have. They are miserable with their lot. They resent that God
has not given them more. Maybe for you it is your spouse.
You are discontent with your marriage. You look around and
see others who are fulfilled in their marriages—but you are
not. They are so affectionate—but he is not. They are so
conversational—but he never says a word. There is no
communication. He ignores you. He never pays attention to
you. She always has headaches and is tired. You might as
well be a potted plant, you say.

The hymn writer writes,

> When peace, like a river, attendeth my way
> When sorrows like sea billows roll;
> Whatever my lot, Thou hast taught me to say,
> It is well, it is well with my soul.

'Whatever my lot,' the Lord is in it. 'It is well with my soul,'
no matter where I find myself. Your relative poverty, your
broken relationship, these things are God's doing. He has His

purposes in them. He has called you to live in these circumstances. Do you believe it? Does it not make a difference? It certainly did for Horatius Spafford, for whom the occasion of authoring these words was the news that his four daughters had been lost at sea! Utterly devastated by this unspeakable tragedy, he writes, 'It is well with my soul.' Why?

He knows the Lord has His purposes in it.

If I were a soldier, I think I could live in a foxhole for several years if I knew that it was temporary and it was for a worthy cause. I'd need to know that the commanders had placed me there in order to fulfill a needed function, but having that confidence, I could do it. This is our situation exactly. Our suffering is temporary, it is a result of the tactical wisdom of our Commander, and it is for our good and the good of the Cause. Our deprivation is His schoolmaster. That husband of yours—that mute, that non-communicative, sluggard of a man is yours by divine providence. That dripping faucet, contentious wife is yours by the hand of God. Now let God's purposes be worked out in your divinely ordered circumstances.

But there is a second problem. You may know and agree that God is in it but you may nevertheless be fighting God. You may be resisting and resenting His will. You can't understand *why* he would deny you the things you want. You can't believe that he could possibly require that you remain stuck with that awful man. You can't believe that He could possibly want you to remain poor. But you read your Bible and you see what it says. And so you grow resentful. You become embittered. You refuse to trust Him. Contentment requires that we not only *know* that God is in everything, but that we *trust* Him as well. Can you trust that as you do the right thing and suffer deprivation (emotional, material or otherwise) He will bless you, and that all loss is merely temporal? Why are you so discontent? The sovereign God who is Goodness itself has called you into your circumstances. It is not an accident. It is not bad luck. These are His purposes for you. Believing this and trusting God is the key to your peace and contentment. Francis Ridley Havergal wrote,

> Every joy or trial falleth from above,
> Traced upon our dial by the Sun of Love.
> We may trust Him fully, all for us to do;
> They who trust Him wholly, find Him wholly true.
> Stayed upon Jehovah, hearts are fully blest;
> Finding, as He promised, perfect peace and rest.

Sovereignty and hope

'When I am weak, then I am strong,' Paul says (2 Cor. 12:10). This statement reflects a holy optimism. 'Yes, I am weak,' he says. 'I have this affliction. It limits my mobility. The pain fogs my thinking. Its unseemliness causes others to turn away. It seems to have a debilitating impact on my ministry. But the opposite is the case. My very weakness is the opportunity for God to demonstrate His power.'

Calvinism is a religion of fundamental optimism. The contentedness of the previous point is not a fatalism. It doesn't breed passivity in the face of adversity. Ours has been an active, resolute, even defiant, tradition. Ours is not like the world's optimism, however. The world urges a positive outlook for the future on the baseless assumption of human goodness and human potential. Auschwitz forever reminds us of the groundlessness and futility of that hope. Our hope rests in a sovereign God. Nothing is impossible for Him.

'With God, all things are possible,' Jesus said (Mark 9:23). This gives me confidence and hope in the midst of shadows and darkness. I am resolute in the face of defeat knowing that God is able even to raise the dead.

Maybe I am old like Abraham. He looked at his body and realized that it was 'as good as dead,' nearly a hundred years old. He contemplated as well the deadness of Sarah's womb (Rom. 4:19). And yet, says Paul,

> ...with respect to the promise of God, he did not waver in unbelief, but grew strong in faith, giving glory to God, and being fully assured that what He had promised, He was able also to perform (Rom. 4:20-21).

This is the point. The circumstances are contrary. The evidence is overwhelmingly negative. What are we to do? We remain resolute, 'being fully assured that what He has promised He is able to perform.' You may be hungry; He can multiply the loaves. You may be sick; God can heal. You may be dying; God can raise the dead. Your family may be falling apart; He can and will reconcile all things.

Our tradition has produced people of great resolution and hope. We think of the Scottish Covenanters who, for decades, suffered at the hands of the British crown. Few people remember anymore that Daniel Defoe, author of *Robinson Crusoe*, also wrote the *Memoirs of the Church of Scotland*, chronicling the fearsome cruelties suffered by Presbyterians resisting Prelacy, suffering which he regarded as being more severe than that inflicted on the Early Church by the Roman emperors or on the Reformers by the Spanish Inquisition. When 1688 brought the deposing of James II and toleration for Presbyterians, twenty-eight years of persecution had brought 18,000 of their countrymen death, exile, or imprisonment. Why had they persevered? They had hope born of confidence in a sovereign God. When freedom finally came, did they curse God for having deserted them for all those years? No! They were confident that their suffering had been the will of God, and from it He would bring greater things.

As for America, we might think of our Pilgrim fathers. They left England in the confidence that God had called them to establish a new civilization. One hundred and two embarked. By the end of the first winter only fifty-five remained, including only four of the original seventeen wives. They managed to plant their crops in the spring and had a successful harvest in the fall. Their response? Did they pack up their things and go home? Did they conclude on the basis of their adversity that God had abandoned them? No! They celebrated their harvest with a day of thanksgiving! They received their suffering as His chastening and continued in the hope that better days were ahead.

Ian Murray's *The Puritan Hope*, among the most inspiring books I've ever read, chronicles the motivating force that Puritan (Calvinistic) optimism has been. Thousands of the early missionaries went overseas and labored for decades with little result. Yet they continued on and on. Why did they do it? They were confident that God had called them there and that eventually He would do great things. My favorite example of this is the father of the modern missionary movement himself, William Carey. Carey worked in India for five years without a single convert. When finally Krishna Pal converted, Carey said, 'He was only one, but a continent was coming behind him. The divine grace which changed one Indian's heart, could obviously change a hundred thousand' (p. 141).

If you are a Calvinist, you must be an optimist. One convert signals the conversion of the whole continent. God can save that lost friend. God can heal that hopeless marriage. God can cure that destitute drug addict. God can do anything, and as Paul went on to say in Philippians 4, 'I can do all things through Him who strengthens me.' I can live with adversity. I can have peace amidst turmoil, joy amidst suffering. I can overcome my lusts. I can conquer defects in my character. I can gain victory over my anger. I can overcome my shyness and cowardice and serve Christ with boldness in public! All the flaws and failings of my personality, all the hardships and imperfections of my environment, all the conflict and dissension in my relationships can be overcome because we serve a sovereign God. In Christ Jesus we are 'more than conquerors,' says the Apostle (Rom. 8:37).

Maybe you're saying now, 'I've believed all this for years, but I've never been called a Calvinist.' Well, it really doesn't matter what you've been called. The labels are irrelevant. The important thing to realize is the basis for your convictions. If you've rejected in theory the teaching we've explained regarding the sovereignty of God, but have been affirming in practice God's role in your circumstances, you have only been able to do so on the basis of inconsistency and borrowed theological capital. If you've believed correctly that 'God has a purpose in such and such a tragedy,' recognize that it is only possible to be consistent by saying, with us, that this is because God is sovereign in all circumstances and at all times and places. Maybe you're beginning for the first time to realize that the convictions that have sustained you in adversity, that have given you a positive outlook on life, are indeed those which affirm the absolute sovereignty of God, those of the Augustinian-Calvinistic tradition. If so, we congratulate you in discovering who you are. And we say welcome to the fold. May your outlook be shaped by the consistent application of these principles. As a sinner who deserves nothing, I thank God for our every God-ordered circumstance. As a child of God, I am content with every particular. As one trusting in a sovereign God, I rejoice in the great things He will yet do.

5

WITNESS

Please read Matthew 11:25-30

Each year our church holds a 'World Missions Conference,' for the purpose of raising support—prayer, financial, and personnel—for the task of world evangelization. The question that skeptics might raise in light of this series of studies is, quite simply, why? Why bother? If God is sovereign, if he has a chosen people whom he has elected from the foundation of the world, then what difference does it make whether or not we evangelize? Doesn't the doctrine of God's sovereignty mean the death of evangelism? Doesn't it destroy all incentive for Christian witness, locally and abroad?

Why, then, do we evangelize? For the same reasons other evangelicals do. Does our Calvinism make any difference in our evangelism? It makes a great deal of difference, as we shall soon see.

Why we evangelize
The Reformed Faith faces no peculiar problems with respect to evangelism. The problems we face are the same that others face. The reasons why we evangelize are those which others express.

First, *we are commanded to evangelize*. However one might interpret the meaning of the doctrine of predestination, it should not affect one's obedience to the Great Commission. No matter what election means, one is still called to obey God, and He has commanded us to,

Go therefore and make disciples of all the nations, baptizing
them in the name of the Father and the Son and the Holy
Spirit, teaching them to observe all that I commanded you;
and lo, I am with you always, even to the end of the age'
(Matt. 28:19, 20).

It would be unbelieving rationalism and sheer disobedience
to allow logic to take over one's thinking and to reason that
since God has already determined everything, we are free to
ignore this command. The same book that teaches
predestination instructs us to evangelize. No matter what we
understand predestination to mean, we cannot allow it to
nullify the mandate to witness. We witness because we are
commanded to witness.

Second, *We live with an antinomy.* J.I. Packer defines an
antinomy in his book *Evangelism and the Sovereignty of
God*, as 'an appearance of contradiction,' and 'an apparent
incompatibility between two apparent truths.' 'An antinomy
exists,' he further explains, 'when a pair of principles stand
side by side, seemingly irreconcilable, yet both undeniable'
(p. 18). He cites the example found in modern physics which
describes light as consisting of both waves and particles
which, on the basis of what we now know, is impossible. It
must be one or the other. But the evidence is there that it is
both, and so it is treated as both. This is how we treat
predestination and evangelism. We offer the gospel freely to
all, even though we know that only the elect will respond.
Why do we do this? For two reasons.

1. Because *the Bible* does it. The Bible itself lives with this
antinomy and never bothers to stop to explain it. Over and
over again, we find side by side the doctrines of grace (e.g.,
God's sovereign initiative, man's inability, predestination,

etc.) and the universal call to all to believe. We can give a number of examples from among the most beloved evangelistic texts, many from the lips of Jesus Himself. You know the famous, 'Come unto me,' passage. This is commonly cited as evidence that God doesn't predestinate. Since 'all' are invited, all must be able. Since 'all' are invited to come, none can be excluded by election. Here is the text:

> Come to Me, all who are weary and heavy-laden, and I will give you rest. Take My yoke upon you, and learn from Me, for I am gentle and humble in heart; and you shall find rest for your souls. For My yoke is easy, and My load is light (Matt. 11:28-30).

The verses that precede it are what is often ignored. Yes, 'all who are weary and heavy laden' may come, but it is also true that Jesus led into this statement with a prayer in which he said,

> At that time Jesus answered and said, 'I praise Thee, O Father, Lord of heaven and earth, that Thou didst hide these things from the wise and intelligent and didst reveal them to babes. Yes, Father, for thus it was well-pleasing in Thy sight. All things have been handed over to Me by My Father; and no one knows the Son, except the Father; nor does anyone know the Father, except the Son, and anyone to whom the Son wills to reveal Him' (Matt. 11:25-27).

Jesus says that the Father 'didst hide' gospel truth from some (the wise and intelligent) and 'didst reveal' it to others ('babes'). Why did He do it? Because it was His will. It was 'well pleasing' in His sight. Further, Jesus says that no one knows the Father except the Son 'and anyone to whom the Son wills to reveal Him.' *Then* Jesus says, 'Come unto me!' It is remarkable. He speaks of the Father hiding truth from some and revealing it to others. He says that one's knowledge of the Father is dependent upon the willingness of the Son to reveal Him. The Son, it is safe to surmise, is willing to reveal the Father to some and not others. The Son does not reveal the Father to all. For some, the truth remains hidden, while for others it is revealed, and the difference is the sovereign will of God, that which is 'well-pleasing' to the Father.

How do you reconcile these things? You don't. How can the invitation to '*all* who are weary' be sincerely offered when He has just said that God is hiding the truth from some? It can, and is. You believe both sides and live with them.

We find another beloved evangelistic text in John 1:12:

> But as many as received Him, to them He gave the right to become children of God, even to those who believe in His name,... (John 1:12)

'Look at the universalistic language,' it is said. 'The offer of the gospel is to "as many as received Him". All are welcome. None are excluded. If predestination were true, it would say, "to all the elect when they receive Him...." This proves that predestination is not true,' it is claimed. Please go on and read the next verse.

> ... who were born not of blood, nor of the will of the flesh, nor of the will of man, but of God. (John 1:13)

How did those who believe and receive Christ come to do so? They were born again. How did they come to be born again?

It was *not* by the 'will of man!' They were sovereignly regenerated by the agency of God. They were 'born... of God.' He spiritually raised them from the dead and brought them to life. Thus, the 'as many as received Him' is limited by 'born...of God.' Can one sincerely say 'as many as received Him' are saved and then turn around and say, in effect, that only those who are born 'of God' will receive Him? The Bible can and does.

Another parallel text which deserves attention but which we shall only mention in passing, is the beloved 'you must be born again' passage. Notice that when Nicodemus tries to find out how he can accomplish this rebirth, he is told he can't. It is not a matter of the 'flesh' (human agency). 'That which is born of the flesh is flesh, and that which is born of the spirit is spirit.' One must be 'born of the Spirit.' Further confusing Nicodemus about 'how to do it,' Jesus says,

> The wind blows where it wishes and you hear the sound of it, but do not know where it comes from and where it is going; so is everyone who is born of the Spirit. (John 3:8)

Can you determine where the wind will blow next? You have as much control over your spiritual birth as you do over the wind. Who controls the wind? God alone. Yet 'you must be born again' (John 3:7). You are commanded and responsible to see that it happens. God is sovereign; you are responsible. How do you reconcile these things? You don't.

Let's try again. One of the most cherished statements of Jesus is found in John 6:35:

> Jesus said to them, 'I am the bread of life; he who comes to Me shall not hunger, and he who believes in Me shall never thirst' (John 6:35).

Again, we see the universal invitation to Christ. He says, 'he who comes to Me shall not hunger.' But look at what follows. Some did not believe what He said. Some took offence. He comments on this:

> 'But I said to you, that you have seen Me, and yet do not believe' (John 6:36).

Then He classifies them as outside of the number of those given by the Father. Election explains their unbelief.

> 'All that the Father gives Me shall come to Me, and the one who comes to Me I will certainly not cast out' (John 6:37).

No, He won't exclude 'the one who comes to Me.' Everyone who comes is kept. But who comes? Those whom the Father 'gives.' Twice again on this occasion, Jesus responds to unbelief by describing the unbelieving as non-elect (as we might call them). First in verse 44:

> 'No one can come to Me, unless the Father who sent Me draws him; and I will raise him up on the last day' (John 6:44).

Then in verse 65:

> And He was saying, 'For this reason I have said to you, that no one can come to Me, unless it has been granted him from the Father' (John 6:65).

The unbelieving are those who cannot come to Jesus and will not unless the ability to do so is given by the Father. He 'draws;' belief is 'granted.' Yet all may come!

We've seen this antinomy in Romans 9–11 already, where Paul moves from 'it does not depend on the man who wills or the man who runs, but on God who has mercy,' to 'whoever calls on the name of the Lord shall be saved' (Rom. 9:16; 10:13).

We'll use as our last example one of the most widely used evangelistic texts found in the Bible, the Parable of the Sower, as found in Mark 4:3-20. Jesus first gives the parable (vv. 3-9), and then explains the parable (vv. 13-20). He explains that the soils represent responses to the gospel: hard soil indicates hearts which the gospel doesn't penetrate; rocky soil, those which the gospel penetrates only superficially and are overcome by affliction; thorny soil, those which receive the gospel but have it soon choked out by worldliness; and good soil, those which receive the gospel and bear fruit. So far, so good. But wait a minute! We've skipped over verse 13. There, Jesus explains the purpose of parables. You thought that he taught in parables in order to illustrate and illuminate the truth? Try again.

> And as soon as He was alone, His followers, along with the twelve, began asking Him about the parables. And He was saying to them, 'To you has been given the mystery of the kingdom of God; but those who are outside get everything in parables, in order that while seeing, they may see and not perceive; and while hearing, they may hear and not understand lest they return and be forgiven.' And He said to them, 'Do you not understand this parable? And how will you understand all the parables?' (Mark 4:10-13).

He taught in parables that the prophesy of Isaiah 6:9 might be fulfilled, that the people might see and hear the truth but not understand, 'lest they return again and be forgiven.' How do you explain? We don't, and neither does the Bible! The Bible, on all these occasions, indicates that God is sovereign in salvation; He chooses some and passes by others, and yet all people are responsible to respond. It doesn't explain how this can be. It merely asserts that it is. So do we.

2. Not only do Calvinists but *everyone else* also lives with the antinomy as well. They just don't admit it, to themselves or others. How so? Only the rankest forms of Arminianism would deny that God has foreknow-ledge and, as we have seen before, the distinction between foreknowledge and foreordination will not hold when dealing with Omnipotence. If God foresees who will believe, then it is certain that they will believe and cannot but believe. If this is so, then we are right back to the problem of predestination. God is bringing people into the world that He knows will never believe, yet He does so anyway. If it is certain they will believe, why evangelize? If it is certain that others will not believe, why evangelize? There is nothing we can do to alter the situation, to effect the outcome one way or another. Even the Arminians, who think they don't have to live with this mystery, do. It can only, ultimately, be avoided by atheism.

Third, *we believe in means*. Calvinism is not fatalism. A fatalist is described above. He believes that what is going to happen is going to happen, and so he gives up and watches. What goes by the name of 'hyper-Calvinism' (but is not Calvinism at all) falls into this trap.

'Hypers' deny the need to evangelize, saying, as John Rylands, Sr. was reputed to say to William Carey as he founded the first modern missionary society, 'Sit down, young man! When God is pleased to convert the heathen, He will do it without your aid or mine!' This is fatalism. It is a denial of the necessity of means. God ordains the ends. But He also ordains the means to the ends. The means to the end of converted sinners is prayer and the preaching of the gospel. There is mystery in this. But our responsibility is not to limit our obedience by our understanding. Our responsibility is to submit our hearts to the command of God and go to all the world with the gospel of Jesus Christ, and pray for its conversion. We do so trusting that He will use our witness and that we shall find, as did the early church, that 'as many as had been appointed to eternal life believed' (Acts 13:48). Through our witness and intercessions, God will gather His elect from the four corners of the earth.

The real question is not 'why evangelize' or 'why pray,' but 'why get out of bed in the morning?' Does God know if you are going to go to work or not? Can anything happen but what He has foreseen? No. Then I guess you can lie there and see how the day unfolds, and if nothing happens, it must be God's will? Since God has ordained from the foundation of the world which shoes you will wear, you can lie still and wait for the right pair to jump on your feet? Of course, this is foolish. The means of getting to work is getting out of bed. God ordains ends *and* means. The same reason why you get out of bed explains why you evangelize. There are means to proper ends.

The difference Calvinism makes
So far we have seen that a Reformed rationale for evangelism is the same as that taken by other Evangelicals. Now we want to look at the advantages that come through the Calvinistic convictions. 'Wait a minute,' you say. 'Did you say, "advantages"?' Yes, I did. It's obvious from the texts we've seen that the doctrines of grace don't detract from evangelism.

But beyond that, there are critical advantages that come to those who believe in the sovereignty of God. They are spiritual advantages, but they are advantages, nonetheless.

First, *the doctrines of grace teach dependence upon God.* What are we saying about a sinner? We are saying that he cannot convert himself, and we cannot convert him. The making of a Christian does not lie in the natural ability of the preacher or the listener. God must convert him. Because men are dead in sin and lovers of darkness, it takes a miracle to make a Christian, a miracle that only God can do. For us to be 'successful' in ministry, we must depend upon God to change hearts. If our theology said a little less than this, for example, that man is only sick and not dead, then we might not have to depend on God so much. We can give medicine to the sick. But we emphatically cannot raise the dead. We could persuade those who have the ability to repent and believe to turn to Christ. But we cannot argue a corpse out of its grave.

Okay, then how do we get God to do it? Answer: through the ordained means. Preach the gospel, live the gospel, and pray. We could say more, especially about worship and the sacraments, but this is an adequate summary for now. If we will concentrate on these things, we will have a much greater likelihood of seeing a significant work of God than we would otherwise. Why? Because these are *the means* He has given to grow His church. Thus, this may be *the* crucial conviction for truly successful evangelism, and here's why.

1. Confidence in ordained means will guard us from *distraction*. Nearly every day I get in my mail an announcement of some new technique, some new program, some new method of growing the church. There are seminars galore. What do they teach? They teach you to work on a number of

'common sense' items which may help your ministry. Work on appearances, they say. Be sure that your facilities are clean and neat. Work on organization. Borrow from the methods of Wall Street and big business. Work on image. Let Madison Avenue ensure that you project the right image to the world. Work on your program. Have something for everyone, young and old, married and single, divorced and remarried, athletic and handicapped. Enormous energy is now being expended by the churches in these areas. This is how we can grow the church, it is thought.

Nothing is inherently wrong with any of this. The problem with it is that it is a tremendous distraction. If all the energy, thought, and time that is being put into these things (demographic surveys and all) were being put into proclamation and prayer, there is no doubt that the church would be ahead. It is scandalous when these external things are the focus in churches which give almost no time to prayer, and little time to preaching. These other activities are not irrelevant, but they come close to being irrelevant when measured by the gospel itself. It is the gospel which is the power of God. The 'style' of a church can be comically poor and God can still bless it. Paul said of his preaching,

And when I came to you, brethren, I did not come with superiority of speech or of wisdom, proclaiming to you the testimony of God ...And I was with you in weakness and in fear and in much trembling. And my message and my preaching were not in persuasive words of wisdom, but in demonstration of the Spirit and of power, that your faith should not rest on the wisdom of men, but on the power of God (1 Cor. 2:1,3,4,5).

He was content with weak methodology because its very weakness provided the black backdrop for the gospel diamond to sparkle more clearly. God's power is 'perfected in weakness' (2 Cor. 12:9). When we are weak we are strong, because our work is more convincingly supernatural when human strength is absent. The faith of the Corinthians might have rested on 'the wisdom of men,' had Paul preached with stylistic finesse. Because he didn't, they saw not a clever man but a 'demonstration of the Spirit and of power.' When we concentrate on the simple, basic means and don't worry about the glitter, people can't say, 'They were successful because of such and such a program or technique.' They will, instead, conclude that God must be in it, and they will truly believe because their faith will not 'rest on the wisdom of men, but on the power of God.' His message?

For I determined to know nothing among you except Jesus Christ, and Him crucified (1 Cor. 2:2).

'Christ crucified' is the message that manifests the power of God. Because God is sovereign we should concentrate on proclaiming it and praying the power of God into it. God, in a moment of revival power, can do more than all our organizing and programming efforts can accomplish in a lifetime. Revivals are born in prayer meetings, not boardrooms. This conviction will keep us focused and on track.

2. Confidence in ordained means guards us from the temptation to use *coercive methods*. A significant amount of today's mass evangelism leans on psychological ploys in order to produce decisions. A great deal of attention is paid to the mood that is set at these meetings. The environment must be 'non-threatening,' warm, and upbeat. Attractive

music and attractive people are paraded to the microphones to help establish the proper setting for the message. Following the message, a decision is called for, and then encouraged by a mass movement of people forward, often inaugurated, by 'counselors.' This herd movement is crucial in turning the will of the unconverted. Multiple stanzas of soft music such as 'Just As I Am,' are played, extending the time given to respond and the psychological pressure.

The problem freely admitted by those who are engaged in this kind of meeting (and the many, many churches that mimic this style in their weekly services) is that many of those who 'decide for Christ' soon fall away. The percentage that become true disciples of Christ is very, very low. Our explanation for the fallout rate is that many of the conversions are psychological only, responses to the various non-spiritual pressures being applied; i.e., the *emotional* (music), the *social* (the herd), and, depending on what message is given, the *carnal* (desire for 'fire insurance', solving of personal problems, etc.). The antidote is unadorned gospel preaching. The gospel itself, apart from its wrappings, is the 'power of God unto salvation' (Rom. 1:16). The Holy Spirit must persuade the heart and turn the will if a person is to be truly converted. Everything else is a counterfeit.

3. Confidence in ordained means guards us from *compromise*. If you are convinced that only God can convert a sinner, that He does so through His gospel message, then you won't be tempted to equivocate when the message is rejected. When the world responds to the gospel with complaints that it is 'too hard,' or 'too serious,' or 'too negative,' which has always been the world's response, the temptation to water-down the message can be enormous. Many ministries have been reduced to entertaining goats, as

William Still calls it, rather than feeding sheep. 'Let goats
entertain goats,' he says, 'and let them do it in goatland.'[1]

Paul warned of this in his own day:

> For the time will come when they will not endure sound
> doctrine; but wanting to have their ears tickled, they will
> accumulate for themselves teachers in accordance to their
> own desires; and will turn away their ears from the truth,
> and will turn aside to myths (2 Tim. 4:3,4).

His answer? 'Preach the word... reprove, rebuke, exhort, with
great patience and instruction' (2 Tim. 4:2). He said of his
ministry:

> ... we have renounced secret and shameful ways; we do not
> use deception, nor do we distort the word of God. On the
> contrary, by setting forth the truth plainly we commend
> ourselves to every man's conscience in the sight of God
> (2 Cor. 4:2, NIV).

The conviction that God is sovereign does this for one. One
looks to God and not human ingenuity. One is not tempted to
make the gospel more palatable to worldlings. One knows
that it is unpalatable. This is expected. One knows that the
unregenerate heart is hard. One knows that it cannot understand
what we're saying (1 Cor. 2:14). What are we to do then?
Proclaim the gospel. It is the power of God. It is 'living and
active and sharper than any two-edged sword.' One can trust
God to work through His appointed means without
manipulating the audience or the message. God encourages
Paul to continue in Corinth saying, 'I have many people in

---

1. William Still, *Work of the Pastor*, p. 8.

this city' (Acts 18:10). They were not yet converted, but they would be. The gospel itself would be the means of digging them out. I believe the same is true for us today. We don't need to use psychological pressure. It doesn't work anyway. We don't need to tone down the message. We would weaken its effectiveness by doing so. What we need to do is depend upon the God-appointed means and get out of the way.

Sadly, the popularity of gimmicks in the churches reveals a lack of faith in the gospel. Behind the dog and pony shows is a lack of faith in the God who gave the gospel. When people again begin to believe in the sovereignty of God, I suspect a lot of these novelties will pass from the scene. The program of the churches will be scaled back and simplified. We will preach, pray, and watch the mighty hand of God at work.

Second, *the doctrines of grace encourage and motivate the evangelist.* Rather than destroying the incentive for evangelism, the doctrines of grace have often motivated the servants of Christ to proclaim the gospel in what have sometimes seemed impossible situations. Why? Because God can change anyone's heart. If the 'heart of the king' is in the hand of the Lord, and He turns it where He wishes, and the king is the ultimate in personal sovereignty, always doing his own will (exactly the Proverb's point), then God can turn anyone's heart—the Apostle Paul's—anybody's (Prov. 21:1). This conviction has emboldened men to stand for the truth in the face of ridicule, violence, and death. It has given them confidence of success amidst hostility, apathy, and incomprehension at home and abroad. Here is the difference. The Arminian preaches with the vision of Christ meekly knocking at the door of the heart of the sinner. Jesus waits. The evangelist waits. Nothing can happen until the sovereign will of man allows God to help. A hard heart can look

particularly hopeless in these circumstances. The Calvinist
has a different image altogether. His Jesus is not passively
waiting. He kicks the door down. There is no door that He
cannot kick down. He can save anyone at any time!

Over the centuries, the greatest Protestant evangelists and
missionaries have been Calvinists. The sixteenth century
Reformation itself, above all else, was a religious revival. Its
leaders were more than theologians. They were primarily
preachers of the gospel and evangelists. Yet, most of them
were Augustinians. The great Puritan preachers of the
seventeenth century were all Calvinists. John Bunyan was a
Calvinist. The greatest evangelist who ever lived, George
Whitefield, the star of the eighteenth century Evangelical
Awakening, was a Calvinist. The other men of the 'Great
Awakening' era, excepting the Wesleys (whom Packer,
nevertheless, calls 'confused Calvinists'), were Calvinists.
We think of the Welshman Howell Harris, the American
Presbyterians, Williams and Gilbert Tennant, the great
Jonathan Edwards, Daniel Rowlands, and many others. In the
nineteenth century, the English Baptist, Charles Haddon
Spurgeon, and the saintly Scotsman, Robert Murray
McCheyne, were Calvinists. Even in the twentieth century,
admittedly not the most successful era for Biblical Calvinism,
Bill Bright, founder of Campus Crusade for Christ, and D.
James Kennedy, author of the Evangelism Explosion, are
both Calvinists.

As for missionaries, virtually to a man all of the founders
of the modern missionary movement were Calvinists. One
can begin with the father of modern missions, William Carey,
and his fellow laborers among the Baptists. They were all
Calvinists. The non-conformists, Robert Morrison, missionary
to China, and Robert Moffat, missionary to Africa, were

Calvinists. The leaders of the missions movement in the Church of England, Henry Venn, John Newton, Richard Cecil, and Thomas Scott, were all Calvinists. In Scotland, John Wilson, John Anderson, Alexander Duff, David Livingstone, John G. Paton and the other pioneer missionaries were Calvinists. It is a remarkable thing, yet true. Rather than undermining evangelism and missions, Calvinism seems to promote it. Whitefield's biographer, Dallimore, suggests that this was true of Whitefield for the very reasons we're stating. He preached with the confidence that God 'is able to save to the uttermost.' He can change a human heart.

I have been ordained to the gospel ministry for over fifteen years now. There have been a number of people during those years about whom I have thought, 'They'll never be reached.' Maybe you have been aware of such people in your own circle of ministry. You may have a gospel-hardened sibling or parent, child or neighbor. You are tempted to think of them, 'They'll never be converted.' You are tempted to give up on them.

Never give up. You may ask my wife: I never give up on people. Why? Not because I'm such a magnanimous person. I don't give up because I believe in the sovereignty of God. God can save anyone. Jonathan Edwards once wrote a *Narrative of Surprising Conversions.* We've seen some surprises. We continue to witness, from the pulpit and the pew, week-in and week-out to hard hearts and hard heads because, if they are to be saved, it is the gospel which will do it.

Does Calvinism make a difference? Oh yes, it does. It forces us to depend upon God and not ourselves. It gives us confidence and hope in the task of gospel witness. And I am convinced that when revival comes, it will be these convictions which will lead the way.

6

SANCTIFICATION

Please read Romans 6:1-11;7:7-8:4

Several years ago a young college student came to me at a social function and began to talk of his spiritual experience. Before long, I could see that he was troubled by something. He related to me his intention to go to Israel so that he might 'feel closer to God.' When I said that I was concerned that he was on the road to deep disappointment since closeness to God has nothing to do with geography, his face took on the look of despair. 'What is it that is troubling you?' I asked. Finally, he unloaded his burden. He said,

> When I became a Christian I was told that I would have an 'abundant life.' I would have peace and joy and would be happy. I was, for a while. But to be honest, I have found the Christian life to be difficult. I struggle with sin and with faith. Because of the struggle, I don't have the joy I should. People tell me that I'm not a good witness because of my despondency. It all makes me want to give up. It's not working for me. So I thought that if I went to Israel I might find the secret of the Christian life.

How would you have counseled this person? Were his expectations (of ease) reasonable? Was his experience (of struggle) indicative of a defective Christian life? The questions we raise here are these: How are those who are saved to make progress in the Christian life? What is the way forward? What can we expect? What must we do to grow daily in the love and knowledge of Christ? Is it through strenuous efforts? Or is it through no effort? Is it something I do, or something God does? Is it through conformity to the law, or through ridding ourselves of the law? Is there a secret to it, or a special formula for success? Or is it something more ordinary and difficult?

Anselm of Canterbury, the first theologian to articulate clearly the 'satisfaction' view of Christ's atoning work, said often of his detractors, 'You have not yet considered how great the weight of sin is.' Anselm said that this was the problem with those who reduced Christ's death to a matter of moral influence. It is also the problem with those who reduce sanctification to an instantaneous experience, or to a special act of faith, or to a matter of mystical contemplation, or to a mechanical process (as in 'spiritual breathing'). They don't understand how much there is to overcome. Sanctification has to do with becoming holy. It means to be set apart morally and spiritually. It means to become Christ-like. How does it happen? Here again, the Reformed faith makes a vital practical difference. Some say, 'You can't do it,' and invite complacency and carnality. Others say, 'You can do it' and invite self-righteousness and Phariseeism. The Reformed faith splits the difference. On the one hand, it rescues us from legalism and moralism (as though holiness were a matter of moral effort alone), and on the other it saves us from false expectations of ease. It captures the balance of God's sovereignty and man's responsibility so powerfully described in Paul's exhortation to, '... work out your salvation with fear and trembling; for it is God who is at work in you, both to will and to work for His good pleasure (Phil. 2:13,14). 'God is at work' and yet we 'work out (our) salvation.' God does it, yet we do it. God is sovereign, yet man is responsible.

The power of sanctification — the Holy Spirit

Jesus said, 'apart from Me you can do nothing' (John 15:5). Only as we are united to Christ can we amount to anything spiritually. The 'we can do it ourselves' crowd needs to hear this and take it seriously. Apart from Him we never will. How may we be united to Him? The Holy Spirit unites us to Christ. How does He do this? First, by regenerating us, then by working faith in our hearts. Faith unites us to Christ and His benefits. This has been generally understood as regards to justification. 'In Him,' Paul says, 'we have redemption through His blood, the forgiveness of our trespasses' (Eph. 1:7). But it is also true of sanctification. He is our 'sanctification' (1 Cor. 1:30). How so? In two ways.

First, in Christ *the power of sin has been broken*. The Holy Spirit unites us to Christ in His death to sin. This is the Apostle's point in Romans 6:

> For if we have become united with Him in the likeness of His death, certainly we shall be also in the likeness of His resurrection, knowing this, that our old self was crucified with Him, that our body of sin might be done away with, that we should no longer be slaves to sin... (Rom. 6:5,6).

The 'old self was crucified with Him.' The 'body of sin' was 'done away with' (*katargeo* = make ineffective, powerless, idle; abolish, wipe out, set aside). What does this mean? Look at the result. God's purpose in uniting us to Christ in His death is 'that we should no longer be slaves to sin.' The goal is that we should 'walk in newness of life' (Rom. 6:4). The old enslaving power of sin has been broken in Christ. A new kind of life is now possible.

The writer to the Hebrews uses the same word in saying,

Since then the children share in flesh and blood, He Himself likewise also partook of the same, that through death He might render powerless him who had the power of death, that is, the devil (Heb. 2:14);

He 'partook' of our nature (i.e., was united to us in our humanity) that he might 'render powerless' the devil. This He has surely done, with the result,

... and might deliver those who through fear of death were subject to slavery all their lives (Heb. 2:15).

We have been liberated from 'slavery.' We are no longer slaves to the devil, fear, sin, and death. Their power has been broken. 'For sin shall not be master over you' (Rom. 6:14).

But thanks be to God that though you were slaves of sin, you became obedient from the heart to that form of teaching to which you were committed, and having been freed from sin, you became slaves of righteousness (Rom. 6:17,18).

Those who are born again by the Spirit of God are delivered from the enslaving, overpowering, tyrannizing power of sin. They have experienced, in John Murray's words, 'a radical breach with the power and love of sin.'[1] John expresses the result of the change categorically:

No one who is born of God practices sin, because His seed abides in him; and he cannot sin, because he is born of God (1 John 3:9)

---

1. John Murray, *Redemption Accomplished and Applied*, Eerdmans, p. 143.

For whatever is born of God overcomes the world; and this is the victory that has overcome the world—our faith (1 John 5:4)

We know that no one who is born of God sins; but He who was born of God keeps him and the evil one does not touch him. (1 John 5:18)

The effect of the new birth is freedom from habitual sin (the meaning of the Greek present tense—'he cannot sin'— means he cannot habitually or characteristically practice sin). The regenerate one 'overcomes the world.' Elsewhere, Paul says, one who is 'in Christ' is 'a new creature; the old things passed away; behold, new things have come' (2 Cor. 5:17). We have a new freedom, a new liberty, and a new master in Christ.

Second, in Christ *the power of God is given.* Not only has something been taken away (the power of evil), but something else (the power of God) has been given. God has given us His Spirit, and 'where the Spirit of the Lord is, there is liberty.' Moreover,

But we all, with unveiled face beholding as in a mirror the glory of the Lord, are being transformed into the same image from glory to glory, just as from the Lord, the Spirit (2 Cor. 3:18).

Notice the passive tense. We 'are being transformed.' By whom? This is the work of the Spirit. Likewise, Paul prays, 'may the God of peace Himself sanctify you entirely' (1 Thess. 5:23). God sanctifies. This is something He does. Do you wish that you were more loving? More joyful? More at peace with yourself? More patient? More self-controlled?

These are all fruit *of the Spirit* (Gal. 5:22-23). The Spirit produces these things.

The Calvinistic/Augustinian tradition says more clearly than any other that we cannot live the Christian life in our own strength. We are too corrupt, too weak and too foolish.

When one joins a Presbyterian church, one promises 'to endeavor to live a life that becomes a follower of Christ.' If this were all that the vow stated, it would be a dangerous vow to take. But this promise of obedience is prefaced by the statement that one does so 'in humble dependence upon the grace of the Holy Spirit.' The vows of membership recognize that we cannot do these things *in our own strength*. Luther wrote,

> Did we in our own strength confide,
> Our striving would be losing;
> Were not the right man on our side,
> The man of God's own choosing.
> Dost ask who that may be?
> Christ Jesus, it is He;
> Lord Sabaoth His name,
> From age to age the same,
> And He must win the battle.

'*He* must win the battle,' Luther says. This is where sanctification begins. Some people are making the mistake of trying to live the Christian life in their own strength. And they are failing. This may be you. You may have been trying for years to overcome your sins. But you have failed. Your temper is out of control. Your lusts are consuming. You have no patience. You still love the world, 'the lust of the eyes and the lust of the flesh.' You care about the things of the world and the opinions of the world. You are often indifferent about the things of God. You can take church or leave it. You can take Bible teaching, prayer, fellowship, or leave them. You have no burden for the lost. Often you hate these things about yourself. You want to gain victory over them and you just don't have the ability. You want to be a better Christian, but you can't seem to do it.

The Reformed faith helps us here. Take seriously your own depravity. Don't be naive about your own potential. You cannot live the Christian life in your own strength. It is not a 'bootstraps' kind of thing. If you think you can, 'you have not yet considered how great the weight of sin is.' Sin is too strong. Depravity is too pervasive.

Some forms of Christian and sub-Christian thinking has sown confusion among many in the church. Because they have minimized sin, they have reduced Christianity to a system of morals. In their extreme forms, Christ becomes just an example for our lives, not a Savior. We don't need a Savior, they say. What we need is an example. Once we have that, we are able to follow the example and live properly. Even the more moderate forms of this line of thinking, which still acknowledge that we need a Savior, so exalt human ability and man's will that they imply that man is able to reform himself—to trust Christ and obey Christ. The Reformed faith agrees that the Bible does have a system of morals and Christ is an example, but says you can't live the system or follow the example. Your heart must be changed first. Then it must be filled with the Spirit of God. The first question raised by the failure to grow in Christ is, are you *in Christ*? Have you been born again? Is the Holy Spirit dwelling in you, changing your desires? This is what the Spirit does, invariably and infallibly. Is He? Go back to the first principles. Have you given yourself completely to Jesus Christ? Is He your Lord and Savior? Only if He is can you ever expect to gain victory over sin, character flaws, and foolishness.

Maybe you are a Christian. But have you consciously drawn upon the power of the Holy Spirit? Sanctification is an act of faith in that one must trust God for it. That trust is expressed in prayers for strength and help, in Bible study and meditation, in use of the means of grace. 'Because I believe that I am weak and You are strong, I pray, O Lord, that you will help me. Give me the power and wisdom I need to serve you.' On the basis of that prayer one then opens the Bible, comes to church, and seeks out the fellowship of other believers. Why? Because we believe what God says about us. We are weak. We must have His strength if we are to succeed. Are you doing these things?

I pray with a prayer list. At the top of my list of petitions is a group of character qualities I'd like to see in myself. I'm too impatient. I'm not sensitive enough. I need wisdom. How am I going to get victory in these areas? Only as I ask God for strength, and use the means of grace faithfully. The bottom line is that *we can't do these things ourselves.* 'If we in our own strength confide, our striving would be losing.' If we are to win, 'He must win the battle.'

The process of sanctification — warfare

So far, we have seen that sanctification is a work of God. He breaks the power of sin. He gives us His strength. It is at this point, however, that the 'other side', the 'God alone does it' crowd makes a mistake. They read in their Bibles all that we have just seen and realize, 'But I still struggle with sin. Its power has not been broken. I do not experience as I think I should the power of God in my life.' So they begin to seek the missing ingredient in their Christian experience. In the last 150 years there has been no shortage of people ready to supply that ingredient for them. Some have seen sanctification as happening through a special act of faith, whereby one might 'reckon' oneself 'dead to sin' (Rom. 6:11). When sin is properly 'reckoned,' one experiences sanctification by faith at that moment, even as one experienced justification by faith at a moment in time.

Others imagine that through the passive act of yielding to God one may be sanctified. According to this scheme, the whole problem with most Christians is that they are striving. What they must do is stop striving. They must yield themselves to God, 'let go and let God.' Only as they do this will they reach a 'higher life,' experience a 'victorious life,' or an 'abundant life,' as it has variously been called.

Still others imagine a second work of the Spirit subsequent to conversion. Sometime after one is saved and one receives the Spirit the first time, one may receive the special empowering of the Spirit, sometimes called the 'baptism' or 'filling' of the Spirit.

These teachings, all designed to eliminate the struggle with sin, give rise to unrealistic and damaging expectations. Each of these views attempts to minimize the struggle inherent to the Christian life. Like the fellow mentioned at the outset of our study, people can be led to believe that if they only had enough faith, or could properly yield, or 'reckon' or receive the 'filling' or 'baptism,' they would be catapulted onto a higher plane of Christian living, above all the struggle and effort being experienced by all the rest. Life becomes for them a constant struggle (ironically enough) to find that plane, and few, if any, ever do. The reason they don't is clear. Without getting into all the exegetical details (see John

Stott's *Baptism and Fullness*, J.I. Packer's *Keeping in Step With the Spirit*; B.B. Warfield's *Perfectionism*), the basic problem is a misconception of what we can expect as Christians in this world. The truth is as follows.

First, the process of sanctification is just that, a *process*. Unlike justification, sanctification (becoming holy and Christlike) does not happen in a moment of time. It is not an instantaneous event. It is, rather, a day by day process of growth in grace. Justification is a matter of being *declared* righteous, as in a law court. Sanctification is a matter of *experiencing* righteousness in one's character and conduct, of *actually becoming* righteous. Daily and progressively, we die to sin and become more righteous.

Second, the process of sanctification may be characterized as *warfare*. We can agree that many Christians fail to avail themselves of the resources that are theirs in the Holy Spirit. We can agree that some who labor joylessly and in defeat need to know that in Christ we are more than conquerors. But the answer is not to avoid the reality of conflict and struggle but to admit it. Confront it head on. This, in fact, is the biblical picture. Vigorous, even violent action is required if we are to gain victory over sin. J.C. Ryle, in his classic study entitled *Holiness*, says, 'A holy violence, a conflict, a warfare, a fight, a soldier's life, a wrestling are spoken of as characteristic of the true Christian.' He cites the 'tried and approved' teaching of *Pilgrim's Progress* as the classic expression of the Christian life.[2] His was a life of continual conflict.

But what does the Bible say, you ask? Well, listen. Let Scripture speak to you. The Bible says we are to 'put on the full armor of God' and in the same passage refers to 'our struggle!' There's the despised word—'struggle.' We are in

---

2. J.C. Ryle, *Holiness*, pp. xvi, xvii.

a 'struggle' with the 'world forces of this darkness....' We must 'take up' our armor. We must 'stand firm.' We are to 'be on the alert with all perseverance and petition' (Eph. 6:11-18). It is expected that we have 'crucified the flesh with its passions and desires' (Gal. 5:24). This requires violent action on our part. Jesus taught that if our right eye offended, we were to pluck it out, and if our right hand offended, we were to cut it off (Matt. 5:29,30). We are to 'consider the members of (our) earthly body as dead' to sin, and 'put them (our sins) all aside', and 'put on the new self' (Col. 3:5, 8, 10). Nor is this to be a one-time effort. It is continuous. 'If by the Spirit you are putting to death the deeds of the body, you will live' (Rom. 8:13). We are likened to soldiers, athletes, 'hard-working' farmers, workmen, bond servants (2 Tim. 2:1-24).

Paul's own experience is instructive in this respect. He likens his Christian life to that of a race which he runs to win, and a boxing match which he fights, likewise to win. He says,

> ... but I buffet my body and make it my slave, lest possibly, after I have preached to others, I myself should be disqualified (1 Cor. 9:27).

Then there is Romans 7. There is considerable argument about whether the experience of verses 14ff is that of Paul before or after his conversion. I am convinced that it describes Paul after his conversion, because he wished to do good and even says, 'I joyfully concur with the law of God *in the inner man*' (7:22). The inner man of the natural man cannot even understand the things of the Spirit of God, never mind rejoice in them (1 Cor. 2:14). I believe that he is describing the fight of faith that the Christian experiences. He wants to do right, but he fails. Indeed, he says, 'I am doing the very thing I hate'

(7:15). What is happening? The dregs of sin, the remnants of sin that remain within him still plague him. Galatians 5:17 may be the perfect commentary on Romans 7:

> For the flesh sets its desire against the Spirit, and the Spirit against the flesh; for these are in opposition to one another, so that you may not do the things that you please (Gal. 5:17).

My first encounter with Romans 7 occurred in college at a time when I was struggling to live the Christian life. Ironically, I was reading a book advocating 'Higher Life' methodology. Several pages into the booklet verses 14ff were quoted, and the words leapt out at me.

> For that which I am doing, I do not understand; for I am not practising what I would like to do, but I am doing the very thing I hate.... For the good that I wish, I do not do; but I practice the very evil that I do not wish (Rom. 7:15, 19).

I thought to myself, 'That is me!' It perfectly expressed what I had experienced in my Christian life. I had been led to believe it would be easy. I had found that it was tough. The world was going in the other direction. The flesh plagued me. The devil badgered me. With Paul, I wanted to cry out to God,

> Wretched man that I am! Who will set me free from the body of this death? (Rom. 7:24)

Now read the next verse, and don't stop with 'Thanks be to God' either. Read the whole verse.

> Thanks be to God through Jesus Christ our Lord! So then, on the one hand I myself with my mind am serving the law

of God, but on the other, with my flesh the law of sin (Rom. 7:25).

Rabbi Duncan used to tell his people, 'You'll never get out of Romans 7 as long as you are at my church.' The 'Higher-Lifers' were saying, 'We've got to get out of Romans 7 and into Romans 8. 'Not under my ministry you won't,' he was saying. The Reformed Faith repudiates all forms of perfectionism. You will never arrive. You will never escape conflict, struggle, or hardship until you are in glory. Paul clarifies any confusion about this regarding himself, saying,

> Not that I have already obtained it, or have already become perfect, but I press on in order that I may lay hold of that for which also I was laid hold of by Christ Jesus (Phil. 3:12).

Sound grim? No, it's just realistic. 'I press on.' That is the key to sanctification. The goal is perfection. You'll never make it in this life. But with the help of the Holy Spirit, we press on toward the goal. We aim at the end—conformity to Christ.

The Reformed faith makes a significant practical difference in the matter of sanctification, as we have seen. Its pessimism about human nature produces a strong emphasis on dependence upon the Holy Spirit. Yet, it does so without being unrealistic about what is required of us. Sin will not be overcome, even in the redeemed heart, without strenuous effort. There are no magic formulas. There are no hidden 'secrets.' There are no special 'keys.' God is at work. He must be, or there's no hope for us. But we also must 'work out our salvation.' If there is a key, it is this: Work it out, struggle, fight—*because* God is at work.

7

ASSURANCE

Please read Romans 8:12-17, 28-39; 1 John 2:3-11

Ours is an age of theological, practical, and experiential confusion. There is scarcely a doctrinal subject that we can consider without hearing a dozen voices calling out in a contrary direction. Our current study is not an exception. Are you sure that you are saved? Leaving aside for the moment the universalist sentiment that the whole concept of being 'saved' is quaint and misguided (because, of course, we *all* are), there are two poles between which the discussion occurs. The first answers the question saying, 'Assurance? I don't think I could ever say that I "know" that I am saved. That would be presumptuous. I hope that I am, but I don't have any certainty about it.' He thinks that he *shouldn't* presume, and neither should you.

The second answer, if I may characterize it, is, 'Of course I am saved – I walked the aisle, didn't I?' Counselors who advise seeking souls from this perspective will say, 'All you need to do is pray this prayer to receive Christ. Once you do that, you can have perfect assurance that you are eternally saved. Do you see the promises of God to those who believe? Do you believe? Then, to doubt it for even a moment is to call God a liar. You don't want to do that, do you?' Instant, easy assurance is given to all, without exception and without delay.

Both answers have problems. Both are contrary to historic

Reformed and Biblical teaching and practice. The first denies the possibility of assurance which the Bible clearly teaches is possible, desirable, and even expected. The second fails to deal adequately with professions of faith in Christ which appear genuine but are not. Our generation has seen millions of 'false professors,' as the Puritans called them, lulled into spiritual sleep by promises of 'eternal security' while they spend decades in open, carnal rebellion. Ask such if they are saved and they'll answer, 'Oh yes, I'm saved! I'm just not walking with the Lord.' Or worse yet, 'I received Jesus as Savior, but I've not yet *made* him Lord.'

This is a vital matter. For a number of years I personally struggled to gain assurance. The struggle had the effect of both deepening my spiritual thirst and robbing me of the peace and joy I should have had. The children of God should not live in fear of the future. They should *know* that they have eternal life. On the other hand, assurance must not be so easily encouraged and arbitrarily given that the goats and tares live securely in their sin.

How, then, are we to proceed? We will make two points that we will examine under three headings. First, true believers (the 'elect') are eternally secure. Second, it is not easy to determine who is a true believer.

Eternal security

There is only one secure foundation upon which to build the doctrine of assurance, and that is the immutable decree of election. This is exactly what Paul does in Romans 8. Any believer who will stop to think about it will realize that his faith, or his 'decision,' or his anything is a shaky foundation upon which to base assurance. Indeed, this is why assurance is impossible on the basis of Arminian assumptions. They teach that one's decision to believe and follow Christ is the basis for one's salvation. But just as one decided to believe, one can decide not to believe. Just as one gained one's salvation by faith, one can lose one's salvation by unbelief. Assurance is impossible because there is always the possibility that tomorrow one might cease believing. One can have assurance for this present moment but not for the next, which is the same as saying that one cannot have any security at all. Assurance is impossible. This has not kept some from creating a Frankenstein theology (like the monster, made up of bits and pieces from here and there) which insists on free will until one 'decides' for Christ, and then argues that from that point forward one is 'sealed' and secure. If one asks, 'What if I decide not to believe anymore?' they say, 'You can't decide not to believe,' to which we say, 'Where's your free will now, friend?' If free will is jettisoned in favor of divine sovereignty at this illogical and inconsistent point, what is the objection to affirming sovereignty throughout the process of salvation, *like the Bible does*? Where? Let me show you. We understand the Bible to teach the following:

First, *God will preserve His elect*. Salvation is an unbroken chain, a 'golden chain,' as it has been called, beginning with the predestinating purposes of God in eternity. Paul writes,

> For whom He foreknew, He also predestined to become conformed to the image of His Son, that He might be the first-born among many brethren; and whom He predestined, these He also called; and whom He called, these He also justified; and whom He justified, these He also glorified (Rom. 8:29,30).

These words are written to a people suffering persecution.

They need encouragement. They're fearful that they might capitulate to the world under the weight of their pain. So Paul writes to build their confidence. Notice the tenses of the verbs. The English past tense is a Greek aorist, indicating completed action. That which lies in the future, our glorification, is so certain that it can be spoken of as an accomplished fact. We are 'glorified.' The links of the chain of salvation are all certain and sure: those 'foreknown' are 'predestined' are 'called' are 'justified' are 'sanctified' (or 'conformed to the image of His Son') and finally, 'glorified.' He does not say they 'shall be glorified.' They already *are* 'glorified,' so infallible are the purposes of God to save His people. Are you a believer? You are such because God determined to save you, gave you the gift of faith (Eph. 2:8,9), and is preserving you until glory. You are as secure as the eternal and unchangeable purposes of Almighty God.

It is on the basis of this foundation that the Apostle can then ask the vital, rhetorical questions of verses 31-35.

'If God is for us, who is against us?'—Whoever might be against us and might seek to destroy us is irrelevant if God is for us.

'Who will bring a charge against God's elect?'—Since God is the Judge, and Christ intercedes, who would dare?

'Who shall separate us from the love of Christ?'—Who could? The love of Christ for us is anchored in eternity. Nothing in time, nothing in this world could interfere with it or disrupt it. Paul's eloquence is too powerful to disrupt as he makes his case:

> Shall tribulation, or distress, or persecution, or famine, or nakedness, or peril, or sword?... But in all these things we overwhelmingly conquer through Him who loved us. For

> I am convinced that neither death, nor life, nor angels, nor principalities, nor things present, nor things to come, nor powers, not height, nor depth, nor any other created thing, shall be able to separate us from the love of God, which is in Christ Jesus our Lord (Rom. 8:35b, 37-39).

It may be possible to state the security of the believer more strongly than Paul just has, but it's hard to imagine how! Nothing in heaven or earth, absolutely nothing can separate us from the love of God.

Ah, but what if I decide to quit believing? Granted that nothing outside of myself can separate me from the love of God, could something inside of me, say, my will, separate me? We ask you, 'Is your will a created thing?' Doesn't he say, 'nor any other created thing'? If, in spite of all that Paul is saying, I have the power to destroy my soul by falling into unbelief, his words give no comfort at all. Above all else, *that* is the thing I fear. What I'm fearing is that I will lose my nerve because of the pressure of suffering. When Paul says, 'nor any other created thing', he includes us. Nothing, absolutely nothing can deter God in His purpose to save us. Jude says He 'is able to keep you from stumbling and to make you stand in the presence of His glory blameless with great joy' (Jude 24). He is able! Jesus said,

> My sheep hear my voice, and I know them, and they follow Me; and I give eternal life to them, and they shall never perish; and no one shall snatch them out of My hand. My Father, who has given them to Me, is greater than all; and no one is able to snatch them out of the Father's hand' (John 10:27-29).

We are not just secure; we are doubly secure, doubly wrapped in the hands of the Son and the Father. We are, shall be, and cannot but be saved.

Second, *God's people will persevere*. We come face to face again with the tension between God's sovereignty and man's responsibility. God's sovereignty protects and preserves His people in the faith. They will not fall away. He won't let them. What, then, are we to make of all the warnings about falling away and the conditional exhortations about endurance? It is simple really. Don't forget *means*. God preserves His people, but it is not apart from the reality of their own perseverance that genuine believers are preserved. They *will* persevere. They *must* persevere. It is through perseverance that God preserves us. We can also truly state the inverse: through His preserving power we are able to persevere. Jesus said,

> And you will be hated by all on account of My name, but it is the one who has endured to the end who will be saved (Matt. 10:22).

The one who is 'saved' is the same who 'has endured.' Only those who endure are saved. God's preserving power makes perseverance so certain that one can say that anyone who fails to endure will be lost. This means that the image of God dragging us kicking and screaming into heaven is wrong. Similarly, the image of the smug, carnal 'believer,' fat and happy in his rebellion and perversion, is wrong. The decree of election guarantees that those who are saved will continue faithfully to serve Christ.

There is a major epistle in the New Testament devoted to the theme of perseverance. Hebrews repeatedly warns those who are tempted to abandon Christianity (in their case for Judaism) that they must continue or be lost. One must continue in right belief and practice. One must continue in faith, love, and obedience. 'Therefore, let us fear,' he tells them, ' lest, while a promise remains of entering His rest, any one of you should seem to have come short of it' (Heb. 4:1). This leaves no room for presumption. One may 'come short' of God's promised rest for His people. More severely, the writer warns,

> For in the case of those who have once been enlightened and have tasted of the heavenly gift and have been made partakers of the Holy Spirit, and have tasted the good word of God and the powers of the age to come, and then have fallen away, it is impossible to renew them again to repentance, since they again crucify to themselves the Son of God, and put Him to open shame (Heb. 6:4-6).

These are notoriously difficult verses which we cannot examine in detail. What we can see is that there is the possibility of apostasy; some had 'fallen away,' and the key to permanent enjoyment of the gifts of salvation is perseverance. Still more strongly, he warns,

> For if we go on sinning willfully after receiving the knowledge of the truth, there no longer remains a sacrifice for sins, but a certain terrifying expectation of judgment, and the fury of a fire which will consume the adversaries.... It is a terrifying thing to fall into the hands of the living God (Heb. 10:26-27, 31).

Then he exhorts them, and us:

For you have need of endurance, so that when you have done the will of God, you may receive what was promised (Heb. 10:36).

We 'have need of endurance' because it is only when we 'have done the will of God' that we will receive the gospel promises. Are we saying that one can lose one's salvation? No! We are saying that one who fails to persevere demonstrates that he was never elect. John says, 'they went out from us but they were not really of us' (1 John 2:19). The sovereignty of God ensures that His people will persevere. If they don't, it indicates they aren't.

The Reformed tradition has not generally been comfortable with the terminology of 'eternal security' because it neglects this aspect of human responsibility and blunts the power of these warnings. Genuine believers need to be spurred on in faithful discipleship. Hypocrites need to be awakened or driven off. Calvinists have, instead, spoken of the 'perseverance of the saints.' Granted, God's sovereignty guarantees that we will persevere, but still, we must persevere. 'If we endure,' Paul says conditionally, 'we shall also reign with Him' (2 Tim. 2:12). The elect 'overcomes the world'; he is not overcome by it (1 John 5:4). Jesus said,

'If you abide in My word, then you are truly disciples of Mine...' (John 8:31).

The elect are secure. They are 'protected by the power of God' (1 Pet. 1:5). He promises to preserve them. Because He does, they will persevere to the end. This can seem a harsh teaching and, approached from one angle, it is. But it is also reassuring. I *will* persevere! Though weak, and tempted, and vulnerable, and, at times, frightened, I will continue in the faith. God promises to 'keep me from falling.' I will persevere.

Assurance may be difficult

'Eternal security,' as we have spoken of it, is the objective reality which true believers possess. 'Assurance' is the experiential certainty of one's possession of eternal security. One is the fact; the other is the feeling. Contrary to common assumptions, the feeling or sense of assurance may not come easily. We don't mean that this is always the case, or that, for some, assurance is not immediately and deeply experienced. In fact, it seems that God often does give those coming out of particularly strong non-Christian backgrounds a powerful sense of certainty, at least initially.

But the New Testament does not generally lead us to expect that this will be the norm. Indeed, the pastoral problem which we mentioned above, that of counterfeit faith, is so widespread and so prevalent a concern that the need to counter it ensures that true assurance will often not come easily. Pastors should not extend assurance directly and indiscriminately to all professing believers because all who profess do not possess! Repeatedly, warnings are addressed to professing believers and church members to examine themselves and repent, or beware. Here's why.

First, *it is difficult to distinguish the true from the false believer*. The wheat and tares as seeds and seedlings are not visibly different. Only when the wheat bears fruit can it be distinguished from the tares, and even then, in this era, they are inseparable (Matt. 13:24-30). The sower sows seed that is fruitful three times, but two of these are not genuine. Rocky and thorny soil both initially bear fruit, the former even receiving the word 'with joy' (Matt. 13:20). The difference between good soil and these is not apparent to the eye. On first inspection, they seem the same.

Second, *the false believer may so approximate genuine faith as to deceive himself and others*. John dealt with people who made deeply spiritual claims about themselves. They were saying that they had 'fellowship' with God, that they had 'no sin,' that they had 'come to know Him,' that they were 'abiding' in Him, and that they were 'in the light' (1 John 1:6,8,10; 2:4,6,9). John denies that any of their claims were true. The writer to the Hebrews speaks of those who had been 'enlightened,' had 'tasted of the heavenly gift,' had 'been made partakers of the Holy Spirit,' had 'tasted the good word of God and the powers of the age to come,' and had received 'the knowledge of the truth' (Heb. 6:4,5; 10:26). It is hard to imagine a more comprehensive description of Christian experience than this, and yet it was false for some. Lives can even undergo extensive, external change. Peter speaks of those who 'have escaped the defilements of the world by the knowledge of the Lord and Savior Jesus Christ' and yet are 'again entangled in them and are overcome' (2 Pet. 2:20,21). At one point, they had actually 'escaped!' Paul can speak of Demas as 'my fellow worker' (Col. 4:14, Phil. 24), and yet later complain that 'Demas, having loved this present world, has deserted me' (2 Tim. 4:10). Paul speaks of those who were so devoted to him and his gospel that they would have plucked out their eyes and given them to him if he had requested it. And yet, because of their flirtations with heresy, he fears that he may have labored over them 'in vain' (Gal. 4:11). One can progress far in the Christian way and counterfeit nearly every internal grace and external change of life.

Third, *for these reasons the criteria for assurance must be stringent*. Both the self-deceived and the consciously hypocritical must be warned, as must the disobedient. Repeatedly, professing believers, members of the visible church, are sharply warned.

Let me cite examples. Jesus said that not all who say, 'Lord, Lord' (i.e., who make a verbal profession of faith) shall enter the kingdom, but *only* 'he who *does* the will of My Father who is in heaven.' A committed, active believer is envisioned making this call of 'Lord, Lord' to Christ. 'Many,' Jesus said, 'will say to Me on that day, "Lord, Lord, did we not prophesy in Your name, and in Your name cast our demons, and in Your name perform many miracles?" And then I will declare to them, "I never knew you; depart from Me, you who practice lawlessness" ' (Matt. 7:22,23). Paul lists various sinners such as fornicators and thieves and concludes that none of them 'shall inherit the kingdom of God' (1 Cor. 6:10). In Galatians, he argues for four chapters that salvation is all of grace. Then in 5:13, he shifts gear, warning the people not to make grace a license for the flesh. He again lists various sins ('deeds of the flesh' such as 'impurity, jealousy, anger', etc.) and concludes 'those who practice such things shall not enter the kingdom of God' (Gal. 5:21). In Colossians, he lists sins again and warns 'on account of these things the wrath of God is coming' (3:6). In 1 Thessalonians, he deals with immorality and warns that 'the Lord is the avenger in all these things' (4:6). James' teaching is well known. 'Faith without works' he says, 'is dead' (2:26). Most vivid of all is the Book of Hebrews, with the warning that we've already seen, beginning with 'if we go on sinning willfully after receiving the knowledge of the truth there no longer remains a sacrifice for sins, but a certain terrifying expectation of judgment,' and concluding with 'it is a terrifying thing to fall into the hands of the living God'

(Heb. 10:26-31). And one could go on and on.

It has become standard practice in evangelical churches to grant immediate and unqualified assurance to those who make a profession of faith. The result has been, I am convinced, to give assurance to thousands of people who have never truly been converted. Then in order to accommodate them theologically, the category of the 'carnal Christian' was created, a notion unheard of in the history of the church. What is the carnal Christian? The carnal Christian is one who has 'received Christ' but who continues in sin. Rather than calling him what he is—a hypocrite or unbeliever—he is coddled with the hybrid label 'carnal Christian.' Thus, one unbiblical concept gives birth to another.

The question that comes to most of our minds is not theoretical. It is, 'What about so and so?' a lukewarm or backslidden loved one who once professed Christ with zeal but has fallen into disobedience.

Have they lost their salvation? No, because, as we've seen, one's salvation cannot be lost. But again, it is an open question as to whether or not they were ever truly saved. We cannot judge. Only God knows the heart. We pray for them, we encourage them and at times we exhort them. But what we can *never* do is to comfort them, and the New Testament is clear about this. There is no comfort, no assurance anywhere in the Bible for those who have professed or even presently do profess Christ and do not walk with Him. We only find warnings whose barbs are intended to wake up the conscience of the wayward and drive them back into the fold of Christ.

We all sin. We all stumble and fall and fail. But where rebellion (whether subtle or open) has become characteristic of a life, where disobedience or lukewarmness has become habitual, we have forfeited any claim to assurance; and to insist upon calling myself or another a 'Christian' in such circumstances, is not faith but presumption. 'If you love Me,' Jesus said, 'you will keep My commandments.' Or in John's words, 'By this we *know* that we have come to know Him, *if* we keep His commandments' (1 John 2:3ff).

I admit that this may not sound like what you've always been taught. But I would challenge anyone to find any other message in the New Testament. If our loved ones and friends are ever to wake up, we must allow His arrows to fly full throttle, without dying the death of a thousand qualifications, until they pierce to the joints and marrow and awaken a true and lasting faith in Christ.

Assurance is expected

While assurance may not come easily, it is expected that the child of God will be certain of his salvation. John states this as his purpose in writing his first epistle.

These things I have written to you who believe in the name of the Son of God, in order that you may know that you have eternal life (1 John 5:13).

'But I don't know,' you sigh. Perhaps you have struggled with uncertainty for years. You want to experience assurance of your salvation, but it has evaded your grasp. As I noted above, for a number of years I personally wrestled with this question. I didn't feel saved. I wondered if my beliefs were just a matter of habit inherited from parents. It's not that I doubted that the Bible was true, just whether or not it was true *for me*. What can we do to arrive at certainty?

First, *believe the promises of God*. It may seem obvious to say it, but it is sometimes overlooked that assurance is a matter of faith, of believing the promises of God. Do you believe the word of God? Have you repented of your sins and received Jesus Christ as Savior and Lord? Then apply strict logic and assertive faith to the promises made to believers. Does the Bible promise that 'whoever shall call upon the name of the Lord shall be saved' (Rom. 10:13)? Yes. Are you a 'whoever?' Yes. Then are you saved? Yes, again. Does the Bible say that 'whosoever believeth in Him shall not perish, but have everlasting life'? Are you a 'whosoever'? Yes, you are. Do you believe, at least enough to say, 'Lord, I believe, help my unbelief?' Yes, you do. Then, what is the result of your faith? You won't perish. You will be given eternal life. Now *believe* these things. God is saying this about you in His word. Believe Him.

Second, *look for what the Puritans called the 'signs of grace' in your life.* Is there present in your character and conduct evidence of the work of the Holy Spirit? The assumption behind this approach, found pervasively in 1 John, is that true godliness is impossible for the unsaved. Where godliness is present (and increasing!), the Spirit must be present; and vice versa, where there is no godliness, there is no Spirit. If, however, godliness is present, we may reason deductively that the Spirit is present, and where the Spirit is present, there must be genuine faith, regeneration, and election. This is not as complicated as it may sound. John repeatedly and simply argues, 'If *this*, then *that*.'

> *If* we walk in the light... the blood of Jesus His Son cleanses us from all sin (1 John 1:7)
> *If* we confess our sins, He is faithful and just to forgive us our sins and to cleanse us from all unrighteousness (1 John 1:9)

If any one loves the world, the love of the Father is not in him. (1 John 2:15)

Similarly, he argues, 'All who do (or don't do) *this* are *that.*'

Who is the liar but *the one who denies* that Jesus is the Christ? This is the antichrist, the one who denies the Father and the Son (1 John 2:22).

If you know that He is righteous, you know that *everyone also who practices* righteousness is born of Him (1 John 2:29).

No one who abides in Him sins; no one who sins has seen Him or knows Him. Little children, let no one deceive you; *the one who practices* righteousness is righteous, just as He is righteous; the one who practices sin is of the devil (1 John 3:6-8).

No one who is born of God *practices* sin, because His seed abides in him; and he cannot sin, because he is born of God. By this the children of God and the children of the devil are obvious: *anyone who does not practice* righteousness is not of God, nor the one who does not love his brother (1 John 3:9,10).

Beloved, let us love one another, for love is from God; and *everyone who loves* is born of God and knows God (1 John 4:7).

Whoever confesses that Jesus is the Son of God, God abides in Him, and he in God (1 John 4:15).

If someone says, 'I love God,' and hates his brother, he is a liar; for the *one who does not love* his brother whom he has seen, cannot love God whom he has not seen (1 John 4:20).

Whoever believes that Jesus is the Christ is born of

God; and whoever loves the Father loves the child born of Him (1 John 5:1).

For whatever is born of God *overcomes* the world; and this is the victory that has overcome the world—our faith (1 John 5:4).

We know that *no one who is born of God* sins; but He who was born of God keeps him and the evil one does not touch him (1 John 5:18).

Finally, he reasons, 'By this or that behavior or attitude, we know that we are genuine believers.'

And *by this we know* that we have come to know Him, if we keep His commandments (1 John 2:3).

... but whoever keeps His word, in him the love of God has truly been perfected. *By this we know* that we are in Him (1 John 2:5).

We know that we have passed out of death into life, because we love the brethren. He who does not love abides in death (1 John 3:14).

Little children, let us not love with word or with tongue, but in deed and truth. We shall *know by this* that we are of the truth, and shall assure our heart before Him (1 John 3:18,19).

And the one who keeps His commandments abides in Him, and He in him. And *we know by this* that He abides in us, by the Spirit whom He has given us (1 John 3:24).

By this we know that we abide in Him and He in us, because He has given us of His Spirit (1 John 4:13).

By this we know that we love the children of God, when we love God and observe His commandments (1 John 5:2).

Jesus taught John that 'you will know them by their fruits' (Matt. 7:15-20). This is, essentially, what John is teaching. But John was, perhaps, the first to teach that since external fruit testifies to the inward condition of the heart, one's regeneration, and therefore one's salvation, can be known through a reflective act. 'Look at the fruit,' he is saying. 'You understand the gospel. Can the natural man do that? Surely not, it is foolishness to him (1 Cor. 2:14). Is this not a sign that you are saved? You grieve and confess your sins. Do you think that you worked that up from within yourself? You keep the commandments, you love the brethren, you don't love the world, you believe Jesus is the Christ. Can the natural man do these things? Are these not the signs of the Spirit's work in your life and, therefore, are they not testimonies that you are a child of God?' This is undoubtedly what Paul meant for us to do when he exhorted us to 'test' ourselves, 'to see if you are in the faith; examine yourselves!' (2 Cor. 13:5). Likewise, this is the only thing that Peter could have meant when he followed his long list of character qualities with the exhortation,

> Therefore, brethren, be all the more diligent to make certain about His calling and choosing you; for as long as you practice these things, you will never stumble (2 Pet. 1:10).

In other words, one makes one's 'calling and election' sure by looking for the fruit of the Spirit, in character and behavior. This guards us from spurious, presumptuous assurance, the assurance of those who say, 'Lord, Lord,' but have not done the will of the Father.

Third and finally, seek the *internal, immediate witness of the Holy Spirit.* We believe that the apostle was referring to this when he said,

> For you have not received a spirit of slavery leading to fear again, but you have received a spirit of adoption as sons by which we cry out, 'Abba! Father!' The Spirit Himself bears witness with our spirit that we are children of God (Rom. 8:15,16).

I have placed this last because I don't believe that this internal witness happens in a vacuum. He testifies that we are children of God through His word, the means of grace, and through the signs of grace. Some who lack this heavenly witness need to seek it, not through a mystical experience, but through the ordinances of the church. Nevertheless, it is a direct, spirit-to-spirit communication that cannot be analyzed, examined, or explained. J.I. Packer in *Knowing God* refers to an old Scots woman who said 'it's more easily felt than tell't.' We don't know how we know, we just know. The sheep know the voice of the Shepherd. Calvin compared this assurance to the sense of taste or sight. How does one know that the night is dark or that a lemon is sour? We just know; it is self-evident, and self-authenticating truth and as undeniable as existence itself. God grants this spiritual sense to His children. He makes it plain; He makes it obvious and real and unmistakable to them. He gives us the confidence we need to feel secure.

This is the balance of Scripture, and the balance desperately needed by the church. Assurance is the birthright of the believer. The religion of Christ, as explained by the Reformed tradition, makes assurance possible. Did you know that virtually no one spoke of assurance at all until Luther and Calvin came along? I wonder if all the many broad evangelicals who talk about 'eternal security' realize their dependence upon Mr. Calvin? We *ought* to have assurance. We *ought* to seek it. We can be sure that God will give it, too! He will not withhold the security that we need and desire any more than would our earthly parents. But we ought not expect it to come easily. Assurance is that certainty which comes only in connection with a steady, consistent walk with the Lord. Anything less than that may not be assurance at all, but presumption. The saints, if they are saints, must and will persevere.

8

LAW AND LIBERTY

Please read Matthew 5:17-22; Romans 8:1-4

J. I. Packer has called 'balance' a 'horrible, self-conscious word.' For the most part, I agree with that assessment, and find myself bothered by few things so much as the preoccupation with maintaining a 'well-rounded life.' I am annoyed by those professing Christians whose chief ambition is to not get 'carried away,' or step too far outside of the mainstream. I am particularly 'not amused,' as Queen Victoria would put it, by those who are trying to balance *me*.

Yet, we have constantly appealed to the 'balance' of the Reformed faith, finding in its careful, thoughtful theology the cure for what ails the modern believer and the modern church. Its balance between divine sovereignty and human responsibility repeatedly provides the insight needed to keep the Christian life in its proper perspective: humility without degradation, contentment without fatalism, witness without manipulation, sanctification without passivity or legalism, and assurance without presumption. Yet, nowhere is the balance of the Reformed faith more obvious than in the relation between law and liberty.

Much of the popular teaching today about the Christian life fails to mention any standard by which to evaluate or guide our conduct. Typically, these works speak vaguely of 'becoming Christlike.' Moral choices are determined equally vaguely by 'the leading of the Holy Spirit,' or 'doing the loving thing.' Whole systems of theology, both liberal and evangelical, deny any place to the law of God whatsoever, and this in an age that is as completely antinomian as any in the history of the world. There is virtually nothing that this society will condemn, that is, except absolutism. All is permissible except violations of the canons of pluralism. Our society kills in the name of life, defrauds in the name of love, steals in the name of justice. Relativism rules the day. We are completely devoid of standards.

The church has paid a price for its moral obscurity and for what has sometimes been ethical heresy. The church, today, is rampant with antinomianism and carnality, and much of it is in the name of the Spirit, love, and Christian liberty. Lax morals are everywhere. Liberal churches are producing studies which condone non-marital sexual relations of all sorts— premarital sex, adultery, and homosexuality included. In the midst of the greatest crisis the family has faced in two millennia, we find the old-line churches parroting the world's agenda, the very agenda destroying the family! The evangelical churches, unfortunately, are not doing much better. Their theory is better, but their practice is abysmal. Christian TV personalities have stolen money from their supporters, been involved in group sex, and visited prostitutes. Christian people think nothing of cheating on their taxes, stealing from their employer, over-drinking, viewing perversions on television and at the cinema, breaking the Sabbath, and breaking their marriage vows. Challenge any of this and one is labeled 'unloving,' 'judgmental,' and 'legalistic,' or, the most damning of twentieth century indictments, 'insensitive.' Isaiah condemned those who called 'evil good, and good evil' (Isa. 5:20). This is the state of affairs in our church and society today.

The Reformed faith has maintained a balance between law and liberty. It has avoided the moral anarchy of antinomianism and the inevitable result, carnality. It has also avoided the opposite error of legalism and the result, bondage and fear. The answer to the ethical chaos of today is to be found along the following lines of Reformed Biblical interpretation.

A law for life

The Reformed faith has always emphasized the continuity between the Old and New Testaments, seeing the two covenants as being bound together by the one underlying covenant of grace. Thus, we are 'Abraham's offspring, heirs according to promise' (Gal. 3:29).

The Old Testament saints, as well as we, are saved by grace, saved by faith, saved by Christ, *and* required to keep the law. Did they really trust in Christ? Yes, they did, in types and shadows and promises. Their faith was certainly without the clarity of vision which we have on this side of the incarnation, yet it was genuine faith in the Messiah. Thus, Abraham had the 'gospel' preached to him (Gal. 3:8; cf. Gen. 12:3), and he, as Jesus said, 'rejoiced to see My day; and he saw it, and was glad' (John 8:56). Moses? 'If you believed Moses, you would believe Me; *for he wrote of Me,*' Jesus said (John 5:46). David 'spoke of the resurrection of the Christ' (in Psalm 16), said Peter at Pentecost (Acts 2:31). 'Likewise,' Peter said in his second sermon, 'all the prophets who have spoken, from Samuel and his successors onward, also announced these days' (Acts 3:24). The prophets, kings, and priests modeled the prophetic, kingly, and priestly work of Christ, and the sacrificial system anticipated 'the Lamb of God who takes away the sins of the world.' The Old Testament was Christ, grace, and faith-centered, and yet the Law of God regulated the life of the people. Our assumption should be that there is no necessary conflict between law and grace.

This is, in fact, what we find in the teaching of the New Testament. Jesus said,

> Do not think that I came to abolish the Law or the Prophets; I did not come to abolish, but to fulfill. For truly I say to you, until heaven and earth pass away, not the smallest letter or stroke shall pass away from the Law, until all is accomplished. Whoever then annuls one of the least of these commandments, and so teaches others, shall be called least in the kingdom of heaven; but whoever keeps and teaches them, he shall be called great in the kingdom of heaven (Matt. 5:17-19).

Jesus says, 'do not think,' because people were thinking the very thing he mentions. He was accused of advocating the abolition of the law. Using strong language, He emphatically denies that He intends any such thing. He did not come to 'abolish' the Law or the Prophets. He came to 'fulfill.' What does 'fulfill' mean? Whatever 'fulfill' means, it does not mean 'abolish.' That much would seem certain. This, however, has not prevented some from maintaining that indeed He did abolish the law. Others have banished the law to a 'kingdom age' and, in practice, thereby abolished it for this age. However, the straight-forward intention of the clause 'until heaven and earth pass away' is to extend the normativity of the law until the end of history. Jesus is teaching his disciples that the Law shall continue to be authoritative for the people of God until the consummation. At no time will it cease to be. All of the Law, down to the smallest letter or stroke, remains in force until its full purpose is 'accomplished.'

If there is any ambiguity, His meaning becomes clearer as He goes on speaking. Ranking in the kingdom of God at least, exclusion and inclusion perhaps, is determined on how one handles the Law. One who 'annuls' the commandments is 'least' in the Kingdom; one who 'keeps and teaches' them 'shall be called great in the kingdom of heaven.' Jesus expects that until heaven and earth pass away, his disciples will *keep* and *teach* the law of God.

His meaning becomes clearer still in his handling of the Law itself. He cites the sixth and seventh commandments (Matt. 5:21ff), for example, and in each case clarifies, deepens, and extends the application of their meaning. The prohibition of murder applies to more than taking another life, but includes the anger and cursing that lead to it. The prohibition of adultery applies to more than violating another person's spouse, but includes the lust that leads to it. Far from abolishing the Law, Jesus 'fulfills' it by drawing out its true meaning and putting it in its proper perspective. The Law is thereby made to fulfill its intended function as a judge of motive as well as action. The Law is 'spiritual' (Rom. 7:14) and, therefore, concerned with internal attitude as well as external act. *Good Summary*

Traditionally, Reformed Christians have followed Calvin in speaking of a 'third' use of the law. In addition to convicting us of our sins and restraining evildoers, it was given, even principally given, to instruct believers. This is why the law has had such prominence in the Reformed tradition beginning with Calvin and mediated to us through the Puritans and the *Westminster Confession of Faith*. The minds of the redeemed need guidance. A dichotomy should not be set up between the 'word' of God and the 'law' of God. It is all divine instruction which is binding upon believers, (i.e., it is law, not suggestion or recommendation). The word of God is 'a lamp to my feet, and a light to my path.' To 'walk in the law of the Lord' is to walk in the way of blessedness. The word keeps us pure and away from sin (Ps. 119:105,111). It is profitable for 'teaching, reproof, correction, training in righteousness' (2 Tim. 3:16). We are sanctified by the word of truth (John 17:17). We have 'in obedience to the truth purified (our) souls.' (1 Pet. 1:22).

'Well, that sounds legalistic,' one says. What does it mean to be legalistic? Legalism is one of three things. First, it refers to trying to be saved by lawkeeping. Works-righteousness is legalism. Second, it refers to man-made rules that exceed the requirements of Scripture. Those who 'bind the conscience' of other believers with rules not found in Scripture are legalistic. Third, it refers to external conformity to the law without the submission of the heart. Those who are content with mere conformity to the letter without embracing the spirit of the law are legalists. *But it is not legalism to obey God. It is not legalism to eagerly and precisely conform one's life to the law of God.*

'What about the leading of the Spirit?' another asks. 'I thought that in the New Testament we are meant to be led by the Spirit, not by the law.' I wrote a thirty-five page paper in seminary on Romans 8:4. Read that verse, and tell me where the Spirit leads the believer. Paul says God 'condemned sin in the flesh.' For what purpose?

. . . in order that the requirement of the Law might be fulfilled in us, who do not walk according to the flesh, but according to the Spirit (Rom. 8:4).

Walking 'according to the Spirit' results in the 'requirements of the Law' being 'fulfilled in us.' Don't pit the Spirit who gave the law (remember, 'the Law is spiritual') against the Spirit who leads the believer. They are one.

'What about love?', another says. 'I thought we were to make decisions based on what is the loving thing to do, not what a rulebook says?' Our answer is that here, as above, a false dichotomy is being set-up. What the law requires *is the* loving thing to do. Follow the reasoning in Romans 13:8-10:

> Owe nothing to anyone except to love one another; for he who loves his neighbor has fulfilled the law. For this, 'You shall not commit adultery, You shall not murder, You shall not steal, You shall not covet,' and if there is any other commandment, it is summed up in this saying, 'You shall love your neighbor as yourself.' Love does no wrong to a neighbor; love therefore is the fulfilling of the law.

What does it mean to 'love one's neighbor'? What it means in our culture today may have nothing to do with what the Bible means. Hollywood has a notion of love that is antithetical to that of Scripture. Some people use the word to indicate strong emotions, others to mean tolerance of differing lifestyles, others to mean eroticism. One can take the word 'love' and fill it with any content one wants. But if one wants to know what God wants of us, one must go the Bible, and the Bible directs us to the law! 'He who loves his neighbor has fulfilled the law' (v. 8). How? 'For this,' he says, and then lists several of the Ten Commandments. 'For this' is what it means to love. To love your neighbor means you don't commit adultery against your neighbor, murder, rob, or covet your neighbor or his things. In other words, fulfill commandments six through ten of the Decalogue. This is what it means to 'love' one's neighbor, to do 'no wrong' to one's neighbor and thus 'fulfill the law.'

Many Christians fail to understand the function of the Law because they view it through the eyes of the Pharisee and Judaizer rather than the Psalmist. As a consequence, they miss the graciousness of the law. The New Testament polemic against the law has in mind the hard, unloving, insensitive outlook of the legalist, not the law itself. The Psalmist, on the other hand, captures the outlook of the godly as he enthusiastically exclaims,

> O how I love Thy law! It is my meditation all the day (Ps. 119:97).

This is to be our perspective. Listen to him delight in the commandments:

> They are more desirable than gold, yes, than much fine gold (Ps. 19:10).

The point of the Law !

It is customary in many Reformed churches to read the Ten Commandments each Sunday in worship. Why is this done? Because 'through the law comes the knowledge of sin' (Rom. 3:20). Why is it important to be aware of our sin? The conviction of sin leads us to Christ to save us from our sin. It is a tutor, or schoolmaster, that leads us to Christ (Gal. 3:24). But that's not the end of the story. Having come to Christ, He sends us back to the law again to show us our duty. Thus, in Geneva, they read the law *after* they had confessed their sins, driving home the point that the law was given primarily to guide us in our Christian walk.

Christian liberty preserved

The genius of the Reformed view of law is that it corrects the libertines without falling into legalism. Ironically, some of the most legalistic groups have been those who have been most eager to deny the Law any place in the Christian life. Typically, they have abolished the Law while, at the same time, adding a host of extra-biblical requirements, like no drinking, dancing, or movie-going. Their peculiar rules support the observation that man needs a law—if he doesn't have God's, he'll make his own.

The Reformed faith has adamantly maintained that there is Christian liberty in areas outside of the application of the moral law. Every bit as strongly as it has argued for the need of absolute and precise conformity to the Law of God, it has argued for liberty of conscience in areas not addressed by Scripture. No tradition has been so strict and rigid in its use of the Law. No tradition has been so rigorous in banishing the commandments of men. We may use the following examples.

There is Christian liberty in the use of *wealth*. The Reformed tradition has held that wealth is a morally neutral thing. Its indulgent use *can* be idolatrous (Col. 3:5), but it can be enjoyed in a God-honoring way. It can also be given away. Some over-zealous advocates of simple lifestyles have robbed people of moderate means of the ability to enjoy what God has given them. These zealots have been rightly accused of guilt manipulation. They have treated wealth as though it were an absolute rather than a relative concept. Who is rich? The tribal chieftain living in a grass hut? Who is poor? The inner city family with its TV and air conditioning? No one can sit in judgment on another as to how he should use his wealth. It would be legalistic to mandate that all live according to a single standard of living or lifestyle.

There is Christian liberty in the use of *food and drink*. They provide the occasion for the extended treatment of the question of Christian liberty in Romans 14 and 1 Corinthians 8–10 and, in part, Colossians 2:16-23. The Apostle Paul asks,

> If you have died with Christ to the elementary principles of the world, why, as if you were living in the world, do you submit yourself to decrees, such as, 'Do not handle, do not taste, do not touch!' (which all refer to things destined to perish with the using)--in accordance with the commandments and teachings of men? (Col. 2:20-22).

We must absolutely condemn gluttony. We must severely condemn drunkenness. But abuse is not the same as use. Jesus cleansed all food (Mark 7:19). Some may choose to abstain from certain foods because of personal preference. But we have the freedom to eat and drink as we please, even if such foods are not fat-free! Here, too, there is a tendency toward joyless legalism, toward man-made rules that take the spice out of life. Our liberty includes the drinking of alcoholic beverages in moderation. Some have made an idol of total abstinence, and the time has come to smash it. Do we speak too strongly? Man-made laws obscure grace. Paul says those who 'advocate abstaining from foods' are practising the 'doctrines of demons' (1 Tim. 4:1-4). Liberty must be preserved.

There is liberty in *vocational choices*. We can work where we wish to work. Of course, one can't become a Christian prostitute or a 'Christian gangster', as mobster Mickey Cohen wished. But, within the bounds of all lawful and legitimate work, there are no superior or inferior vocations. Those who go into the secular workforce are not missing

'God's best.' All Christians are called to Christian ministry, but not all are called to *vocational* Christian ministry (1 Cor. 7). We have liberty in this.

There is liberty in *leisure pursuits*. One can play sports, enjoy fine music, and read books. One is not required to be laboring always for the kingdom of God. There is, in Christ, the freedom to relax and enjoy the world. Again, this must occur within the bounds of the law of God. One must not turn the Sabbath into a day for secular fun, or find leisure in the immoral. But as the Puritan, Richard Sibbes, said, 'God has created worldly things to sweeten our passage into heaven.'

There is liberty in *marital decisions*. One can choose to marry, or choose not to marry (1 Cor. 7:27ff). The only restriction is that one marry 'in the Lord.' It is absolutely forbidden for a Christian to marry an unbeliever (2 Cor. 6:14ff). But, if you want to remain single, you may. If you wish to marry, you may. If a man wishes to marry Sue and not Sarah, he may. There is freedom in this.

In each of these cases, there is both law and liberty, freedom and form. Grace does not mean license (Gal. 5:13). Freedom is not anarchy. The gospel doesn't abolish standards. 'Do we then nullify the Law through faith?', Paul asks. 'On the contrary, we establish the Law' (Rom. 3:31). Faith defines the proper role and function of the Law and marks out its limits. Faith establishes both the realm of law and the sphere of liberty.

When the relation between law and liberty is not understood, the result is often a plague of guilt feelings. Guilt feelings are only valid when there is actual guilt, the guilt of a guilty record resulting from a transgression of the law of God. When there is such, sin is to be repented of and guilt feelings cast off. But guilt feelings should never be used as a means of positive motivation. If you are sinning, repent. Do what is right because you wish to please God, not because you feel guilty.

Should you feel guilty about having a drink? Not unless it leads to drunkenness. Should you feel guilty about buying a nice car? Not unless the desire for it is idolatrous. Should you feel guilty about not giving more money to the church? Not if you are tithing. What about eating a large, luxurious meal? Is it a sin to eat heartily? Not necessarily. It is only sin if you are being gluttonous. If you are sinning, repent and quit. Get rid of the guilt. There is a great deal of motivation by guilt going on in the church today. Extrabiblical and unscriptural obligations are being heaped up on the backs of people, burdening them with guilt and robbing them of their joy. Frankly, these are the tactics and style of the cult. In cults, everything is governed by a law. Individual freedom is denied and suppressed. Leaders make decisions as to who shall marry whom, who shall do what kind of work, who shall live where. This is bondage. Where you see this or the tendency toward this, flee.

Our question is, is it commanded in Scripture? If it is, we must do it, completely, precisely. If it is not, we are free to do and free not to do, as taste and wisdom dictate.

Order restored

Psalms 19 and 119 list the benefits which come through knowledge of the law. They include wisdom, cleansing, purity, comfort, direction. Live consistently with the moral law of God, and you live wisely. It would be difficult to overestimate the blessing that comes through conformity to the Ten Commandments. A published study of New Haven, Connecticut (where Yale is located) showed that crime had increased between 1960 and 1990 by phenomenal amounts: murders from 6 in 1960 to 31 in 1990; rapes from 4 to 168; robberies from 16 to 1,784; aggravated assaults from 72 to 2,008; burglaries from 567 to 4,476; auto thefts from 475 to 3,459. What is true of New Haven is true, more or less, of the whole country. Crime is epidemic. We are all frightened. The courts and prisons are overwhelmed. Now, the good people are imprisoned in their homes behind barred windows and doors, and the criminals are walking free. Regrettably, as we have seen, the church has not had a united voice in promoting the moral law of God. Theologically, there has been confusion. Actual practice, of late, has been disastrous. While there has not been violent crime in the church, there has been a notorious amount of sexual indiscretion and financial mismanagement. The church, called by the Apostle Paul, 'the pillar and support of the truth' (1 Tim. 3:15), has been a pillar of salt. Yet, every single one of the problems we face in society or church is addressed by the Ten Commandments. The Ten Commandments teach the values which will restore order in our society. Only the Reformed faith has consistently maintained their normativity for today and, therefore, has an alternative to the moral chaos of today. Can this be demonstrated? We think so.

Aren't we in trouble today because of the breakdown of authority, as parents, school teachers and administrators, the police, and our elected officials are all regularly dishonored and defied? Doesn't the fifth commandment establish parental authority and, with it, all human authority under God? Doesn't the law of God require that we honor all legitimate authority and condemn the defiance and disrespect so prevalent today?

Aren't we in trouble today because human life is no longer

regarded as sacred, and with this cheapening of life has come abortion, infanticide, suicide, murder and horror crimes involving mutilation and dismemberment? Doesn't this commandment protect all innocent life and require that society regard all human life as sacred?

Aren't we in trouble today because of the breakdown of marriage? Isn't the root of that breakdown the rejection of the seventh Commandment and its condemnation of all extra-marital sex? Does it not at once establish the basis for preventing illegitimacy, venereal diseases, divorce, broken homes, single parent households, homosexuality, and all the crime that flows from these symptoms? Would not conformity to this one commandment do more to heal this epidemic of heartache and do more to heal the whole social order than any other single principle?

Are we not in trouble today because so few show respect for the property of others, and think nothing of destroying, 'trashing,' and stealing that which belongs to another? Does not the eighth Commandment uphold the sanctity of private property, commanding 'thou shalt not steal,' and requiring restitution when property is destroyed?

Are we not in trouble today because there are so few people whose word we can trust? Isn't the root cause of the 'credibility gap' between the people and advertisers, politicians, businessmen, store-owners, and virtually everyone the loss of the concept of the sanctity of the truth, the principle behind the ninth Commandment?

Are we not in trouble because even those who do obey the law do so in a legalistic and Pharisaic fashion, violating the spirit of the law (and the tenth Commandment), so that our political and legal codes must grow beyond comprehension in order to prevent evasion, giving rise to a legal elite who control the lives of all the rest, all in violation of the tenth commandment which internalizes and spiritualizes the intent or spirit of the law?

Finally, are we not in trouble because we are ethical relativists, having no absolute standard on the basis of which to judge behavior and, therefore, are forced to accept all lifestyles and moral choices as equally valid? Are not Commandments one through four the moral foundation of society because they establish that there is only one God, and, therefore, there is only one truth and one law?

Are not these commandments the outline of the principles that will cure what ails our society and church today? No secular program and no amount of money can overcome the destructiveness of the prevailing moral anarchy.

Thus, to a decadent, antinomian age we restore the Law of God with its absolute standards of right and wrong. Yet, we do so without the bondage of legalism. We do so in a way that maintains the liberty of the Christian and the joy of the Christian life. We say to the church and to our nation, come home to your moral foundation!

9

PRAYER

Please read James 4:1-10

'Why do you Calvinists bother to pray?' it is sometimes asked. 'Since you believe everything is predestined anyway, and there is nothing that you can do to change what God has unalterably decreed from all eternity, why pray? Why pray for some lost soul to be saved? He's either elect or he isn't. Why pray for the sick to be healed? God has ordained their state of health. It obviously won't make any difference.'

These are good questions, aren't they? The larger issue that they raise is 'What is prayer?' What are we doing when we pray? What are we trying to accomplish? What purpose does God have in mind in urging us to pray?

Much of the popular teaching on prayer is fundamentally unsound. Some of it presents prayer as a kind of arm-twisting of God, 'My will, not Thy will, O Lord.' Some of it is little more than the 'vain-repetitions' condemned by Jesus, a Christianized magic designed to coerce favors from a reluctant God. Prayer in practice in these circles is defined as 'intercessions,' and limited to that.

But this is not the worst problem. The fatal weakness of the modern church is not its *view* of prayer but its *practice*, or should we say, its non-practice. The western, modern church is not a praying church. We are an activities church. We have meetings and programs and projects to keep us busy. We have buildings and budgets and organizations and plans to discuss. We have time for virtually everything, including prayers to start and close our activity times, but that's about it. Congregational prayer meetings are a thing of the past. I have no hesitation in saying that the basic problem behind the prayerlessness of the church is unbelief.

No tradition has emphasized prayer more than the Reformed. Prayers for conversions and revival are almost the creation of the Reformed community. There has been no failure of nerve when it comes to vigorous intercession. Yet there is a breadth and depth to the Reformed view of prayer, a breadth that restores to prayer its central place in the life of the people of God. Why do Calvinists pray? Prayer is vital for two basic reasons: it changes us, and it changes history.

Prayer changes us

My own personal prayer pilgrimage reached a point of crisis during my one-month pastoral internship in Scotland in the Spring of 1978. I had received most of my instruction on prayer from para-church campus organizations. We had been taught to pray with prayer lists, which I still do today. But we were also taught, or at least it was implied, that prayer was the means of getting what we wanted from God. We had even been cautioned *not* to pray 'thy will be done.' This was thought to cancel the intent of our prayer. Did we want God to do 'X', or merely to do His will which He was going to do anyway? It seems incredible to me today, but this is what we were taught. Can you imagine wanting anything other than the will of our all-wise, all-good, heavenly Father? Can you imagine preferring your own will, based as it is on your own limited knowledge and outright foolishness, to that of God's? But back to Scotland—one Sunday morning it was my responsibility to lead the entire worship service and to preach. Prior to the start of the service a small group of committed folks met with the pastor to pray for the worship to follow. We were seated in a circle when the time to pray arrived. In unison they all rose, turned around, and got down on their knees. What followed was the most incredible outpouring of prayer that I had ever heard. Most of the praying I had ever done had been of the 'just really,' variety. 'Lord we just really are glad to be here,' etc. Their prayers, however, were impassioned, God-centered expressions of praise, confession, and intercession. 'O Lord, we praise Thee!' 'O Lord, we thank Thee for Thy great grace and love for Thy poor servants;' 'O Lord, pour out Thy Spirit upon the minister of Thy Word this morning;' and on they went.

As the time for prayer drew to a close, I reluctantly anticipated my responsibility to utter the concluding prayer. By this time, I was undone. My trite, chatty, frivolous prayers seemed utterly bankrupt to me. I thought to myself, 'I have no business leading these people in worship—they should be leading me.' I stumbled through my prayer and the service and spent the next six months in a state of crisis, wrestling with whether or not I was truly called to the ministry. Their prayers taught me a great deal about prayer and about myself.

Prayer changes us. How? We can make three points.

First, it brings us to the *posture of spiritual prostration before God.* Prayer is not primarily intercession, but praise. Robert Murray McCheyne said, 'What a man is, is what he is on his knees before God, and no more.' This is the Reformed perspective. There is no God so great as the God of Augustine and Calvin. There is no God so sovereign, so powerful, so awesome, and so inscrutable. Prayer to this God changes our stance in life from autonomous agents of self-will to humble supplicants of Almighty God.

This is how the Bible teaches us to pray. Jesus said, 'When you pray,' (He assumes that we do) 'pray, then in this way,

> Our Father, who art in heaven,
> Hallowed be Thy name.
> Thy kingdom come.
> Thy will be done,
> On earth as it is in heaven (Matt. 6:6, 9,10).

What is the focus of this prayer? The praise and worship of God is the focus. He begins His prayer with praise. It is completely misguided to rush into the presence of God with a shopping list of requests without first giving God His due as God. Jesus praises the heavenly Father, the Father who is upon His throne in heaven, who sovereignly rules from there all that He has created. He is a Father, with fatherly love and authority. His name is to be 'hallowed,' or set apart, for He is holy. His kingdom and will are to be our concern, not our little kingdoms and wills. Jesus is God-centered in His prayer and wants us to be the same. Prayer is not a quick list of 'gimmes' addressed flippantly to God. Prayer is the changing, not of the mind of God but, of our whole orientation from one absorbed with our own concerns, to one focused on God and His glory and will.

Second, in addition to humbling us, prayer changes us by *building our faith*. Review the prayers of the Bible and I think that this is exactly what you will find again and again. The Prophets and Apostles begin their prayers with the praise and adoration of God, partly because by so doing they gain confidence in God's ability and willingness to grant their requests. David's prayer at the time of the dedication of the materials to be used in the construction of the temple began,

Blessed art Thou, O Lord God of Israel our father, forever
and ever. Thine, O Lord , is the greatness and the power
and the glory and the victory and the majesty, indeed
everything that is in the heavens and the earth; Thine is the
dominion, O Lord , and Thou dost exalt Thyself as head
over all. Both riches and honor come from Thee, and Thou
dost rule over all, and in Thy hand is power and might; and
it lies in Thy hand to make great, and to strengthen
everyone. Now therefore our God, we thank Thee, and
praise Thy glorious name' (1 Chron. 29:10-13).

See how he rehearses in God's hearing His own attributes.
God is pleased with this. And as we are saying, it changes
David. David is consumed with the glory of God. This vision
is faith building. The temple must be built. Shall it be? Oh,
yes! This God can do anything!

You will find a similar pattern in Isaiah 37:16, where
Hezekiah, praying under the threat of the Assyrian invasion,
says,

'O Lord of hosts, the God of Israel, who are enthroned
above the cherubim, Thou art the God, Thou alone, of all
the kingdoms of the earth. Thou hast made heaven and
earth.'

He reminds Himself that God is enthroned on the highest of
thrones, 'above the cherubim,' that He is Lord of 'all the
kingdoms of earth,' that He made 'heaven and earth,' and
therefore, He can handle the Assyrians.

Similarly, in Jeremiah 32, the Prophet Jeremiah is promised
that after the Chaldeans invade and Israel is carried off into
captivity, God's people will be restored. He is instructed to

buy land within the city even as the Chaldeans build their
'siege mounds.' He struggles to believe that this is actually
going to take place. What is the sense of this, he wonders? So
he prays:

> Ah, Lord GOD! Behold, Thou hast made the heavens and
> the earth by Thy great power and by Thine outstretched
> arm! Nothing is too difficult for Thee, who showest
> lovingkindness to thousands, but repayest the iniquity of
> fathers into the bosom of their children after them, O great
> and mighty God. The LORD of hosts is His name; great in
> counsel and mighty in deed, whose eyes are open to all the
> ways of the sons of men, giving to everyone according to
> his ways and according to the fruit of his deeds...' (Jer.
> 32:17-19).

His prayer goes on. What is he doing? He is strengthening his
faith. He begins by recalling the power of God in creation and
quickly realizes 'Nothing is too difficult for Thee.' Of course
God can make it all work out.

The early church provides another example. The first
barrage of persecution suffered by the infant church in
Jerusalem resulted in the arrest and detention of Peter and
John, official threats, and a frightened church. What did they
do? They prayed. Luke records for us,

> And when they heard this, they lifted their voices to God
> with one accord and said, 'O Lord, it is Thou who didst
> make the heaven and the earth and the sea, and all that is
> in them' (Acts 4:24).

See how they build their faith at the outset by recalling God's
wisdom and power in creation? Let's face it. It is hard to pray.

We have to beat and flail our flesh to get ourselves to pray and to stick to it once we start. Why is this so? Because of unbelief. What can we do? David, Hezekiah, Jeremiah, and the early church all remind themselves of the greatness and the power of God. They are praising God for who He is. They are humbling themselves before Him. In the process, they are strengthening their faith. Prayer is changing them. They are trying to fortify their faith and believe in the midst of trials that God, the great God, is able to do something for them.

Third, prayer changes us by *cleansing our souls*. This God-centered approach to prayer leads inevitably to the confession of our sins. Isaiah 6 provides the classic example of what happens when one receives a fresh vision of the glory of God. The revelation of the true God, the God who is not just holy, but 'holy, holy, holy,' leads to the cry,

> 'Woe is me, for I am ruined! Because I am a man of unclean lips, and I live among a people of unclean lips; for my eyes have seen the King, the Lord of hosts' (Isa. 6:5).

Prayers of praise lead to prayers of confession. Listen to Daniel as he prays for the restoration to Palestine of the exiles in Babylon:

> And I prayed to the Lord my God and confessed and said, 'Alas, O Lord, the great and awesome God, who keeps His covenant and lovingkindness for those who love Him and keep His commandments.'

To this point, Daniel's prayer is a prayer of praise. But quickly it shifts to confession:

'... we have sinned, committed iniquity, acted wickedly, and rebelled, even turning aside from Thy commandments and ordinances. Moreover, we have not listened to Thy servants the prophets, who spoke in Thy name to our kings, our princes, our fathers, and all the people of the land. Righteousness belongs to Thee, O Lord, but to us open shame, as it is this day—to the men of Judah, the inhabitants of Jerusalem, and all Israel, those who are nearby and those who are far away in all the countries to which Thou hast driven them, because of their unfaithful deeds which they have committed against Thee. Open shame belongs to us, O Lord, to our kings, our princes, and our fathers, because we have sinned against Thee. To the Lord our God belong compassion and forgiveness, for we have rebelled against Him; nor have we obeyed the voice of the Lord our God, to walk in His teachings which He set before us through His servants the prophets. Indeed all Israel has transgressed Thy law and turned aside, not obeying Thy voice; so the curse has been poured out on us, along with the oath which is written in the law of Moses the servant of God, for we have sinned against Him' (Dan. 9:4-11).

Space limitation requires that we stop his prayer at this point, but it goes on in the same spirit for eight more verses! Praise leads to confession. Daniel is changing. He is believing God and rehearsing his and his people's sins and turning from them.

We see the same with Nehemiah. He receives a report of the desperate condition of those former exiles who have returned to Palestine from captivity. They are in 'great distress and reproach, and the wall of Jerusalem is broken down and its gates are burned with fire' (Neh. 1:3). So he responds:

> Now it came about when I heard these words, I sat down and wept and mourned for days; and I was fasting and praying before the God of heaven. And I said, 'I beseech Thee, O LORD God of heaven, the great and awesome God, who preserves the covenant and lovingkindness for those who love Him and keep His commandments, let Thine ear now be attentive and Thine eyes open to hear the prayer of Thy servant which I am praying before Thee now, day and night, on behalf of the sons of Israel Thy servants, confessing the sins of the sons of Israel which we have sinned against Thee; I and my father's house have sinned. We have acted very corruptly against Thee and have not kept the commandments, nor the statutes, nor the ordinances which Thou didst command Thy servant Moses' (Neh. 1:4-7).

Those who approach prayer as though God were a celestial Santa Claus are entirely missing the point. Do you wish to see God do a great work? Might it be something as far-fetched as building a temple (or church), delivering us from an overwhelmingly powerful enemy, delivering us from the grip of an enslaving power, or from persecution? Might it be to see a loved one saved, a friend delivered from drugs, a neighbor healed from a disease? Then quit thinking that the critical thing is changing God. *We* are the ones who must change. This is exactly what James tells his readers.

> You ask and do not receive, because you ask with wrong motives, so that you may spend it on your pleasures (Jas. 4:3).

They were praying, but their motives were all wrong. It wasn't enough to ask; they had to ask in the right way, and doing so meant that they must change.

> Draw near to God and He will draw near to you. Cleanse your hands, you sinners; and purify your hearts, you double-minded. Be miserable and mourn and weep; let your laughter be turned into mourning, and your joy to gloom. Humble yourselves in the presence of the Lord, and He will exalt you (Jas. 4:8-10).

God will hear our prayers and 'exalt' us *if* we are praying as we ought, prayers rich with praise and confession of sin, prayers hot with passionate pleas. Such prayer changes us. It builds our faith. It removes whatever sin-barriers might be present. It creates the kind of conditions under which God is willing to bless.

Prayer changes history

'That's all well and good,' you say, 'but you really have not yet answered the question. Does prayer really make any difference?' Well, now that prayer has changed you and gotten you into a spiritual condition of humility and trust where God is willing to hear your prayer and bless you, the answer is yes, it does. James says it simply,

> You do not have because you do not ask (Jas. 4:2)

Even a child can understand the meaning of that sentence. 'If you had asked, you would have; but you didn't, so you don't.' Asking results in receiving. Failure to ask results in deprivation. Jesus said the same:

And I say to you, ask, and it shall be given to you; seek, and you shall find; knock, and it shall be opened to you. For everyone who asks, receives; and he who seeks, finds; and to him who knocks, it shall be opened (Luke 11:9, 10).

'We non-Calvinists believe that,' the critic responds. 'We want to know why a Calvinist, who believes everything is predestined, believes it. Why do *you* believe that prayer makes a difference?' Let me respond.

First, it is *arbitrary* to raise the issue of the relationship between human responsibility and God's sovereignty at the point of prayer. The question is much more extensive than that. The real question, as we have suggested, is not 'Why pray?' but, 'Why do we get out of bed in the morning?' and it is a question that all theists, not just Calvinists, must answer. All who believe that God foreknows all things, in other words, all Christians, must wrestle with the question as to how anything that we do makes any difference. If God foreknows, as He surely does, then nothing can be other than how God has foreknown it shall be, and nothing we do as a consequence makes any difference. The fact is, there is a mystery in the relationship between human responsibility and God's sovereignty, a mystery that we cannot resolve. God does foreknow and foreordain all things, and we do have to get out of bed and we do have to pray.

Second, prayer should be seen as just *another means* to God's ends, just like everything else in the Christian life. How do people get saved? Through the preaching of the gospel *and* through prayer. How do people get healed? Through the use of medicine *and* through prayer. Prayer changes 'history,' by which we mean not the things famous people do but merely everything. We can give some examples.

Moses prays and a battle goes well. Moses stops praying and the battle goes poorly (Exod. 17:11). Elijah prays and the rain stops for three years. He prays again and the rain starts up again (Jas. 5:17,18). Daniel prays and is told by the angel Gabriel that 'at the beginning of your supplications the command was issued' that would result in the release of the nation of Israel from captivity (Dan. 9:22,23; 10:12ff). 'Oh, but they were exceptional people,' I have sometimes felt. James makes the opposite point. 'Elijah was a man with a nature like ours, and he prayed earnestly that it might not rain, and it did not rain....' (Jas. 5:17). The key is character. It is 'the effective prayer of a *righteous* man' that is blessed. Yet, it 'can accomplish much' (Jas. 5:16). Prayer, you see, accomplishes.

Why does James tell us to 'pray for one another, so that you may be healed,' unless it is true that in response to prayer God heals (Jas 5:16)? Why does Paul ask the Colossians to pray 'that God may open up to us a door for the word,' unless it is that in response to prayer God opens doors of opportunity (Col. 4:3)? Why is it that Paul prays at the beginning of the Ephesian, Colossian, and Philippian letters that his readers may be given 'a spirit of wisdom and of revelation in the knowledge of Him'; that their hearts 'may be enlightened' (Eph. 1:17,18); that they may be 'filled with the knowledge of His will in all spiritual wisdom and understanding' (Col. 1:9); that their 'love may abound still more and more in real knowledge and all discernment' (Phil. 1:9), *unless* it were possible to effect these heart changes, these religious and spiritual changes, through prayer? Why does Jesus promise, 'If you abide in Me, and My words abide in you, ask whatever you wish, and it shall be done for you,' if he doesn't intend to do it for us (John 15:7; cf John 14:13,14; 15:16; 1 John 5:14)?

No, the real question is not why do Calvinists pray, but why do others pray? It only makes sense to pray for God to change a human heart if He is able to do so. If, however, He can be stopped by the human will, if He must be invited to help, if He may only meekly knock and must meekly wait for the door to be opened for Him, then why pray for the salvation of sinners? Don't our prayers assume that God can raise the spiritually dead, give sight to the spiritually blind, and understanding to the spiritually dull? The doctrine of God's sovereignty is an inducement to prayer, not an inhibitor. Prayer is the means by which we see the plan of God put into action. In response to prayer God gets busy.

This is the Calvinistic theory. We pray because prayer changes us. Through prayer we are humbled, we grow in faith, and we cleanse our hearts. We thereby become spiritually ready to receive the blessing of God. James expresses it all in one sentence. We 'confess (our) sins to one another, and pray for one another, so that (we) may be healed' (Jas. 5:16). Confession gets us spiritually ready, and then through intercession actual healing takes place. Prayer is a means. It prepares. It accomplishes.

If this is the theory, then what about the actual practice? Probably it's too much like unbelief. Little prayer goes on. Spurgeon said he prayed like a Calvinist (like it was all up to God), and preached like an Arminian (like it was all up to him). Too often we pray like an Arminian (that is, very little, since it is all up to us, we think) and preach like a Calvinist (with little enthusiasm or feeling, since it is all up to God). What should we be doing? We should strengthen our faith by rehearsing the attributes with adoration in extended prayers of praise. We should remove the last barriers to belief and blessing through the confession of our sins. Then we should assault the throne of grace with our requests. 'Let your requests be made known unto God,' Paul told the Philippians (Phil. 4:6). Having been changed by prayer, we are free to ask for the things we want, with the confidence that God hears and will answer.

What about that unconverted loved one? This one has been exposed to the gospel in the past and scoffed at it. That one has repeatedly said that he is not willing to change or give up his pet sins for the sake of Christ. This other one is indifferent and has been for years. Nothing seems able to spark his interest in the things of God. God, in response to prayer, can change the heart of the most lost of the lost. He can change the heart of the most hardened, the most anti-, the most indifferent unbeliever. Pray the door open. He promises to hear our prayers and do it! Pray down the gates of hell! Pray down the fire of God!

What about that friend that is enslaved to his lusts? What about this other one who is a captive of drugs or alcohol? What about that one whose temper explodes unpredictably and violently? Is there no hope? God, in response to prayer, can change their hearts. He is not impotent before the human will. He need not wait until He is invited. Plead with Him! The power released in prayer can overcome any obstacle.

Then there is your son's, your daughter's, your neighbor's, your friend's, marital problems. There have been moral problems. Perhaps little communication goes on. Finances may be poor. The situation seems desperate. The differences seem irreconcilable. Hearts are being torn to pieces. The wounds are deep and are still bleeding. What can we do to help? This is what we are always asking. What can we do? Here is the answer. We can pray down the reconciling power of God. He can heal any division, and has done so before. He can light a fire under the most sluggish of males and throw ice on the most hot-headed of females. He can put His salve on the deepest wounds and heal them. Pray, plead, believe, God can do the impossible and promises to do so in response to our prayers!

What about the church and the world? Can anything reverse the decline we see in the institutions around us? Will the church ever rise up from the deep sleep in which it now is? Will we ever again see revival sweep the church, with the gospel thundering from the pulpits, the pews filling up with spiritually hungry masses? Will we ever see revival flood the whole nation, bringing the indifferent or hostile masses to a saving knowledge of Jesus Christ? Will we ever see the gospel so touch the nation that robberies become rare and violent crime almost a thing of the past? Will we ever see the time when 'the knowledge of the glory of the Lord covers the earth as the waters cover the sea?' The answer is so simple and accessible that we miss it. Wasn't the early church 'continually devoting itself to prayer?' (Acts 1:14; 2:42) Didn't Pentecost begin in a prayer meeting? Won't a commitment to prayer change us and, in so doing, lead to the changing of the world?

Prayer is the means God has given to us for the changing of the world. Over ten years ago, I attended my first Saturday night prayer meeting at the Gilcomston South Church of the Church of Scotland in Aberdeen. The meeting started at 7:00 p.m. and ended, to my utter amazement, at 10:15! Over three hours of prayer! The praying began with adoration and praise, but before long their intercessions were ranging all over the world. At the time, the 'Boat People' were drowning in the South China Sea by the tens of thousands. Along with the prayers for spiritual revival in the Church of Scotland, there were passionate prayers for the 'poor suffering boat people.' Within a week an international meeting of heads of state was called by Margaret Thatcher, and soon the U.S. Navy was fishing these desperate people out of the sea. I believe the Saturday night prayer meeting had something to do with it. There is no limit to what God might do in our generation. 'We do not have because we do not ask.' Let us, who believe in the sovereignty of God, be about the business of asking.

I recently received a letter from a good friend in Florida, a member of the Granada Presbyterian Church. For nearly ten years now, he has been on the brink of death because of a heart condition.

One December, he had another in a long string of critical incidents. His account of it captures better than anything I could say the meaning of the Reformed view of prayer, as well as the strength that comes from confidence in the sovereignty of God.

I'd like to share one significant incident with you. Last December, on Pearl Harbor Day, I woke up having significant anginal pain. My wife took me straight to the hospital. My heart was unstable all day and became much worse about 5 p.m. so I took my eleventh trip to the cardiac cath lab.

This was a routine emergency procedure that I had been through before, or so I thought! However, somewhere along the way the procedure failed....

Then, all of a sudden, I remember thinking that I was having the most vivid dream of my life. I dreamed I was lying on an operating table in a small room full of people. The people were screaming at each other. The room looked very familiar and I just couldn't believe how realistic this dream was.

A pretty black lady hit me in the chest with her fist as hard as she could! My body shook all over. I felt my ribs cracking from the blow but it didn't seem to hurt. The black lady bent over me, smiled lovingly, and said, 'Mr. Frank, I'm so sorry I had to do that to you!' How strange! Was this a dream or what?

Then someone yelled, 'CLEAR', and I literally received the shock of my life. I smelled burning flesh, I had burning chest pain and a burning chest. I couldn't breathe by myself, my chest hurt so bad!!! They were frantically punching me in the neck and all over my body with needles... bad veins, I guessed. This definitely was NOT a dream; it was a 'code blue' incident!

Again and again, I saw people looking at each other, shaking their heads and saying, in effect, that I was not going to make it, I was going to die! I guessed that all those people, who were obviously trying to save my life, didn't know that I could see and hear them. This was depressing. But wait! All was not lost! God was there with me!!! My wife and my pastor, Jim Smith, the Rupps, the Kerrs, and the Ramseys were in the waiting room praying. The Granada prayer chain would be activated. None of us dies by accident. God would decide the outcome of this incident!!!

The black lady who punched me in the chest and shocked me with the paddles took me by my left hand, leaned over and said to me, 'Do you know Jesus?' I said, 'Yes, how else could I go through this?' Well, I know that is what I said and I know she understood because she smiled that special smile. But I'm not sure I said it with words because my mouth was covered with a breathing bag. Her hand felt warm and strong and my arm started to tingle. I could feel the power of the Holy Spirit moving over me. I felt God was giving me the choice to either go home with Him or go home once again with my family. I chose to stay with my family as I had on other occasions.

Days later, the leader of the cardiac cath team stopped by the cardiac unit to give me his perspective on what happened that fateful night. Dr. Martin very humbly told me that he and the other doctors and nurses felt they could not take the credit for me being alive today. He felt the credit should go to a higher authority... one more powerful than he. How right he was! I thanked him for saving my life for the second time in two years and tried to explain to him that although God saved my life, God used him and his associates and all my brothers and sisters in Christ who were praying to accomplish this miraculous event.

In conclusion, what did God teach me from this incident? God is always present and in control. None of us will ever die by accident without His knowledge or permission. He will take us home at His pleasure!

God responds to our prayers and usually works in our lives through a brother or sister in Christ, like the black lady, and all those Granada prayer warriors. We need to practice, more and more, this powerful, mysterious, privileged activity we call prayer. *I am convinced that it changes the natural course of events as it did on my Pearl Harbor Day.*

When we reach out and take His hand, God will make our pain bearable, our suffering sweet, and give meaning to those events in life that are so difficult to understand.

10

GUIDANCE

Please read Psalm 23

Whom shall I marry? Where shall I live? Where shall I work? These are the three big questions in life. There are dozens of lesser ones that weigh heavily upon us as well. Where shall I go to school? Shall I buy that car? Shall I go on that trip? Answering these questions can sometimes be agonizingly difficult. My decision to become the youth director at Granada Presbyterian Church rather than Bible teacher at a Christian school in Macon back in June of 1982 took several weeks of internal debate and confused prayer. Day after day, I screamed within, 'What shall I do?' Most of you have been in this situation at one time or another. Some others are *always* in this state of mind. We just don't know what to do.

The question that we have to address here is whether or not God can be of any help to us in our decision making. For this, more than on any other subject, we are assuming an evangelical understanding of God and our relationship to Him. We are assuming that God is a personal being who loves His people in Jesus Christ and who promises to guide His people like a Father and Shepherd. We are assuming that it is true that,

He makes me lie down in green pastures; He leads me beside quiet waters. He restores my soul; He guides me in the paths of righteousness for His name's sake (Ps. 23:2, 3).

Again David the Psalmist says,

> Good and upright is the LORD; therefore He instructs
> sinners in the way. He *leads* the humble in justice, and He
> teaches the humble His way.... Who is the man who fears
> the LORD? He will instruct him in the way he should
> choose (Psa. 25:8, 9, 12).

It seems clear enough that *God leads* and *guides* and *instructs*
us *in the way (we) should choose.* The debate that has been
conducted in evangelical circles has been over *how* God
guides His people. How does He make His will known? How
does He communicate the optimum path to take? There are
two extremes to avoid. The first is the excess of the
superspiritual, for whom inner promptings, unusual
providences, dreams, and voices apart from the Word become
infallibly authoritative. A great deal of foolishness has been
done in recent years in the name of what 'God told me to do'
through one of these means. The other extreme to avoid is that
of reducing guidance to nothing more than the application of
Biblical principles. The Bible, in this view, becomes
'blueprints' for life which can be read virtually without
supernatural help. This position tends toward Deism, a
'watchmaker' view of God's relationship to His people,
eliminating any meaningful, personal interaction or
communication between God and His people.

Somewhere between these two positions lies the Biblical
balance. God guides His people. He does so through His
Spirit. Yet the Spirit does His work through sound principles
and, as we'll see, through interpreting our circumstances.

The Spirit's Illumination

The Reformed tradition has firmly denied that God gives to his people any new revelation, 'those former ways of God's revealing his will unto his people being now ceased' (*The Westminster Confession of Faith*, 1.1). Even those who do not agree with this position should be willing to agree that God does not *usually* lead His people by speaking audibly or directly to them. He didn't do this in Bible times, and He doesn't do it now. The average Hebrew farmer who sought God's guidance as to whether to plant wheat or barley was not told directly. He prayed for, and was given, the wisdom needed to make the decision. Likewise, even those who believe in ongoing prophecy and revelatory dreams should be willing to agree that this kind of guidance is the rare exception today as well. Most of our guidance, the everyday variety for everyday people, is much more mundane, even for the charismatically-inclined.

The supernatural role of the Holy Spirit is, nevertheless, still vital. We must have the Holy Spirit if we are to avoid miscalculation and missteps. However, His work this side of the completion of the canon of Scripture should be understood as that of *illumination* and not *inspiration*. The Holy Spirit is the key to guidance, but He guides not by giving to us new information (as in 'Do this or that'), but by illuminating the given word and our circumstances and thereby showing us the path of wisdom. He gives to us a settled peace and certain conviction, assuring us that we are moving in a direction consistent with His good purposes for us. He illuminates all the factors before us so that we are able to choose that which is wise and good.

How does he do this? We have given hints already. For a more complete answer we move on to the next section.

The evangelical principles of guidance
Let's look at how the Spirit does this work. Sound answers
can be found by reviewing the standard evangelical teaching
on guidance.

First, *God guides us through Scripture*. This is true in both
the specific sense of *(a)* forbidding certain options and
prescribing others, and in the more general sense of *(b)*
shaping the desires, outlook, and perspective of the child of
God. For example, if I were seeking marriage, the Scripture
would tell me not to marry a non-Christian, as in 'a.' But, it
would also shape my concept of what marriage is, why
marriage is an 'honorable estate,' and the kinds of qualities
to look for in a wife, as in 'b.' Thus a godly single man will
seek a Christian wife both because this is what Scripture
demands *and* because Scripture has shaped his desires so this
is also what he *wants*, even longs for. If I were looking for a
job, the Scripture would tell me not to look for a job as a drug-
pusher or gangster, as in 'a,' but it would also tell me of the
dignity of labor and to look for work that maximizes my gifts
while serving the church and society, as in 'b.'

In the prescriptive and restrictive senses we read,

> How can a young man keep his way pure? By keeping it
> according to Thy word.... Thy word I have treasured in my
> heart, that I may not sin against Thee (Psa. 119:9, 11).

In the shaping sense we read,

> Thy word is a lamp to my feet, and a light to my path (Psa.
> 119:105).

Paul can say that all Scripture is,

...inspired by God and profitable for teaching, for reproof, for correction, for training in righteousness; that the man of God may be adequate, equipped for every good work (2 Tim. 3:16, 17).

The word of God equips us 'for every good work' by limiting our options and shaping our interests. It teaches us in a positive sense, informing us of the truth and training us in righteousness. It also reproves us, correcting errors and showing us where we are off the mark.

The Bible is the primary means by which God leads His people. More than any other factor, it determines the kind of life that we are going to lead. Literally thousands of options are eliminated by the Bible's influence on us. Nothing that is illegal, immoral, selfish, or unloving can even be considered. But again, it is important to realize that it does this not just by specific rules (our 'a'), but also by giving to us the 'mind of Christ' (1 Cor. 2:16, our 'b'). By the constant reading, study, and meditation upon God's word we begin to 'think God's thoughts after Him,' to use Calvin's phrase. Thus, to be 'filled with the Spirit' is to 'let the word of Christ dwell richly in you' (compare Eph. 5:18,19 with Col. 3:16). To be 'led by the Spirit of God' has specifically to do with mortifying the flesh and walking in the Spirit's way (Rom. 8:12-14).

The Bible teaches us to look at life and its options as God would look at them. As we inwardly digest the word of God, it becomes almost instinctive for us to respond to the world from the perspective that God has, on the basis of divine values and priorities. Many who wrestle with decision making need not look any further than this. More than once I have heard from people in great anguish of soul struggling with whether or not to pursue a divorce when they didn't have

Biblically sanctioned grounds. They asked, 'What does God want me to do?' There is no mystery to the answer in these circumstances. Stay put! The key to the troubles of many is ignorance of the mind of Christ as revealed in His word and illuminated by the Spirit. The key to their relief is knowledge.

Second, *God guides us through prayer*. Are you having trouble making a decision? Have you prayed for guidance? 'You have not because you ask not.' James says,

> But if any of you lacks wisdom, let him ask of God who gives to all men generously and without reproach, and it will be given to him (Jas. 1:5).

Repeatedly, in Jesus' life major decisions were preceded by prayer (Luke 3:21; 5:16; 6:12; 9:18; 9:28, 29; 11:2ff, etc.). As was true of Scripture, we may think of prayer's role in guidance in both a specific and a general sense. One should pray concerning a particular decision, that one will do the wise and God-honoring thing. But there is also the more general reality that it is in the context of praying that God gives us answers. It may even be that we are praying about 'y' when an answer comes clear regarding 'x.' Many, many times I will get the outline for my sermon during my regular morning devotions when I am reading an unrelated passage of Scripture or praying about something else. Just as often, I have received clear, strong convictions about a ministry in our church—that we must do this or quit doing that. In fact, just about every new idea of my pastoral ministry has come to me during my morning prayers. Why would this be the tendency? Because, when we ask, God hears (and answers) and *we* hear. When we pray, we slow down (finally) and listen. When we pray, we are not pumping our minds full of news, music, conversation, entertainment, and so God has an opportunity to speak to us. How many marriages are a mess because husbands and wives are not pausing to pray and listen? How many vocational choices have been foolishly made because people have not been humbled in prayer and patiently waited and listened? Remember, do not minimize the foolishness of the human heart or the thickness of the human skull. We are slow and prone to error. We need the wisdom of God if we are to live wisely. To get it, we must ask.

Third, *God guides us through godly counsel*. Each step of the way in the decision making process ought to include the advice and counsel of the wise. Many times, our strong convictions are half-baked. We've not really thought it all through. There are blind spots in our view of things. We've not considered all the factors. Because a warped perspective is inevitable, it is necessary that we seek the counsel of others. Alone, we are weak. 'But in abundance of counselors there is victory' (Prov. 11:14). Solitude leads to presumption. 'But with those who receive counsel is wisdom' (Prov. 13:10).

The way of a fool is right in his own eyes, but a wise man is he who listens to counsel (Prov. 12:15).

Listen to counsel and accept discipline, that you may be wise the rest of your days (Prov. 19:20).

Without consultation, plans are frustrated, but with many counselors they succeed (Prov. 15:22; cf. 20:18; 24:6).

The Presbyterian system of church government assumes the truth of this principle. Authority is not to be given to any single individual. Rule is collective; power is dispersed. Changes in the status quo come only through collective deliberation. On a regular basis in committees and in the Session we see that wisdom is found in 'an abundance of counselors' as proposals are corrected, altered, improved, and, finally, denied or approved through the collective wisdom of these bodies.

Another area where this principle is well illustrated is in the call to the ministry. The Reformed tradition has seen a distinction between the 'internal' and 'external' calls. The former is one's conviction that one has been gifted and called to preach. But that has never been regarded as sufficient alone. The 'internal' must be confirmed by the latter, the 'external' call given by the church. The church collectively evaluates the sense of call that a candidate has and either confirms or denies it. This serves to prevent unwise decisions which are doomed to frustrate and hurt the ungifted. Regretfully, in the last few years we have seen many a young man go off to seminary, spend three to four years and thousands of dollars being trained, get ordained and serve for several years in the church, and then realize that he doesn't have the gifts. Broken-hearted, financially and emotionally devastated, and, worse, sometimes profoundly cynical about the things of God, he leaves the ministry. The wise man will demand confirmation, knowing the foolishness and deceitfulness of his own heart (Jer. 17:9).

These are the generally accepted principles of guidance in evangelical churches. These are the things that the Holy Spirit uses to guide His people. The Reformed tradition affirms them and, if anything, underscores them because of its more profound doctrine of sin. We must have the guidance of God in our decision making because of our capacity for error. This guidance is given by the Holy Spirit, not through impulses, voices, or dreams, all of which are too subjective for sin-prone hearts, but through the objective criteria of Scripture, prayer, and godly counsel.

The Reformed supplements

While the above principles are vital, they don't go far enough. They miss critical information which the Reformed tradition catches because of its grasp of the sovereignty of God. We can summarize this doctrine with one sentence: God has made you what you are. Through creation, redemption, and providence God has made you what you are. There have been no accidents; He is the author of all the factors. Because He is, we may assume that all of these things work together in indicating the kind of life that God has ordained that I should live. Profound insight into what God *wants* from us may be found in understanding what God has *made* of us.

Let me give an example. When was Paul called to be an apostle? On the Damascus Road, when Jesus appeared to him in a blinding light? In one sense, yes. That was when the call itself was received. But, he tells the Galatians that God had set him apart 'from my mother's womb' (Gal. 1:15). Yes, he had been called 'through His grace' on the Damascus Road. But Paul can look back over the whole of his life and see the hand of God at work. God was preparing him for the work of evangelizing the Gentiles while he was still in the womb, and then all through his development, prior to his conversion, up to the Damascus Road experience.

I have known of people who have been converted as adults and then despised their natural gifts and family background and refused to make use of them. As far as natural gifts and background relate to salvation, Paul regards them as rubbish (Phil. 3:4-8). But he was born with Roman citizenship, and when trapped, he used it (Acts 16:35-40; 25:11). He was trained as a Pharisee, and when cornered identified with them, defending himself as 'a Pharisee, a son of Pharisees' (Acts 23:6). He received a first rate education from Gamaliel and the University at Tarsus, and his use of it is obvious throughout his writing. Thus, when he looks back over the whole of his life, he sees the sovereign God preparing him for his work each step of the way. All the factors were ordained of God to equip him for the task of taking the gospel to Gentiles, the first group of which were attending Jewish synagogues. He understood the thinking of the strictest sect of Judaism and his most vehement opponents, the Pharisees, and later, the Judaisers. Why? Because God had ordained that he should be born into a family of Pharisees. He *knew* the Jewish world. But he was also born into a family of Pharisees living in a Gentile city, Tarsus. Thus, he knew the Gentile world as well. He could speak and write the Greek language; he had been to their schools. He knew their thinking. He read their poets (Acts 17:1ff.). When saved, there were then added spiritual gifts on top of the natural. Creation, Providence, and Redemption were in harmony with each other.

How do you apply these principles? These are the questions I would ask of someone who is seeking God's guidance. Who made you? God? Well then, what has He made you to be? What are your natural gifts? What are your natural interests? Why would God have given to you these gifts and interests unless He intended you to use, even develop, these gifts? Isn't it honoring to the Creator when that which he creates functions to its fullest capacity?

Then, I'd ask a second series of questions. What opportunities have you had? Who has given them to you? Isn't God sovereign over your opportunities and lack of opportunities?

Let me illustrate with my own life. I love to read and study history; I always have. Where does that desire come from? I believe it is just a part of what I am, of how I was created. Some people love mechanical things, some like books. For me, it is history. Because it is inborn, there is no explanation but that God has given it. But then, there were encouraging factors along the way. My father loved war history and exposed me to a great deal of it. My fifth grade teacher, good ol' Mr. Beacon, discerned my interest and knack for it and stimulated me further. Who ordered and determined these factors? The God of providence. Then, when I awakened spiritually, should I have expected that the God of redemption would lead in a direction completely contrary to that which He had been developing all those years? Or would there be continuity and convergence between creation, providence, and redemption? Unless the Creator, Governor, and Redeemer are three different gods, each with different agendas, we should expect harmony. I think I always knew that my vocation would involve the study of history. When I began to discern a call to the ministry, the call came to one who had already discovered that a large part of Biblical interpretation is understanding history, both the historical context in which Scripture was written, and the history of the interpretation of the various passages. The first time I sat down to prepare a Bible study and then actually taught it, I knew I was doing what I was made to do. There was a sense of 'oughtness.' It fit. My whole life had prepared me for that moment and for the tasks of the teaching ministry.

You can say all the same things about yourself. You have natural interests and abilities. There have been opportunities along the way that have nurtured and developed those interests and abilities. When you decide to choose a major in college, then a career, and then a place to live, won't these factors, all determined by the God of creation, providence, and redemption, play a vital role? The gifts and calling of God go hand in hand. What has He made and nurtured you to be? What are your interests? What are your abilities? What are your opportunities? We ask these questions assuming that you are already applying the evangelical principles above. You are in the word of God, praying, and seeking godly counsel. But since you are doing that, ask yourself what has your Creator and Governor, your Father and Friend, made you to be? Are you good with numbers? Pursue them. Are you gifted in music? Develop it. A good organizer and 'doer?' Look for administrative work. Burdened to teach and preach? Exercise your gifts.

We've mainly looked at vocational matters, but the same principles apply to everything. What are your interests? What are your opportunities? Both times that I selected seminaries to attend the decision was long and painful, but finally clear. A silly, superficial Californian needed to get out of the U.S.A. and study under a man of the quality and character of J.I. Packer. It 'fit.' There was a sense of 'oughtness.' The same was true of my return to the USA, to Gordon-Conwell Seminary. There was a convergence of factors which left me one day—I remember the moment—convinced that I must go there. Coming to the Independent Presbyterian Church of Savannah was a similar experience. I love history—here is an historic church. I believe in preaching—here is a high pulpit. I believe in traditional, reverent worship, this is what they wanted. I idolized Scotland—here is a Scottish heritage. I had dreamed of serving a downtown church. It fit. It—dare I use the words—*felt* right.

Examine the marriage question for a moment. How did I

know that I wasn't supposed to marry someone from Northern Germany? Because the Governor of the world never gave me an opportunity to do so. If he had intended me to marry a woman from Northern Germany, he would have arranged it. Instead, he plopped young Emily rather unmistakably into my life. Then He gave me a great love for her. Here is an interesting question. Why do we love the ones we love? Though I wish desperately not to insult my wife, the answer for me and, unless I miss my hunch, the answer for most of us is, 'I don't know!' We just do. Oh, I can talk about her being pretty, intelligent, funny, feisty and so forth. But the bottom line is, I just do. I don't know why I love her. I just do. It has to do with who I am and who she is and how we mix. Therefore, I take these things as clues from the One who made me 'who I am' as to what I ought to do. The Spirit must illuminate our circumstances. He must help us to interpret the creational and providential factors. But when we take the gifts and opportunities and interests that he has given to us and use them for His glory, He is pleased. When Dr. Werner von Braun built the Saturn 5 moon rocket and it took off and performed flawlessly, it honored Dr. von Braun. More than that, it honored the God who made the man who made the Saturn 5. So it is with all our gifts. When we use them, we honor the God who gave them. We know what He wants by what He has made. What He has created us to be is what we are to seek to become.

There is also a liberating freedom in the Reformed view which ends up saying, as Augustine did, 'Trust God and do what you want.' We are not captives of a hidden, 'third' will of God. We have real freedom to do what we want to do because what we want (when we are walking with Christ) has been determined by what God has made us to be. For a number of years I assumed that, if I wanted something, God would not want it for me. I assumed that creation and redemption were at odds with each other. My natural desires, I assumed, were carnal and invalid. This can be a very hurtful and oppressive outlook on life, stifling natural and God-given desires. We are free in Christ to be all we want to be. Certainly this approach is open to abuse. It is easy to seek our own will in the name of God's will. But when we are seeking the Spirit's guidance through the word, prayer, and godly counsel, we will find our desires converging with His. What we want, we are relieved to know, is what He wants. Harmony is the new emphasis. What He has saved us to be turns out to be the same thing that He created us to be. We are freed in Christ to become all that He made us to be.

The Reformed faith is beautifully holistic. It does not limit our endeavors to 'spiritual' things. It doesn't limit God's involvement to supernatural things. All things work together for the good of God's people. He guides us through the totality of His work, His word, His world, with His Spirit leading and illuminating us each step of the way until we come to that place where we become certain that the next step is taken in His wisdom. This sense of 'oughtness' is never infallible. We make mistakes, but it is possible to achieve a high degree of certainty that, when we see creation, providence, and redemption converge, indeed we are walking in the 'paths of righteousness', in the paths He has chosen for us.

11

A FAITH FOR LIVING

Please read Romans 11:33-36

We have come now to the end of our journey into the practical implications of Calvinism. We have highlighted the 'doctrines of grace,' especially the doctrines of God's sovereignty, man's depravity, and sovereign grace. We have sought to demonstrate the application of these doctrines to the various areas of 'practical piety,' and found more than enough that is of critical importance for Christian life and living. Now, it only remains for us to summarize our findings and drive these truths into our hearts and consciousness, the inspiration for which we return to Romans 11:36.

> For from Him and through Him and to Him are all things. To Him be the glory forever. Amen.

Comprehensive
B.B. Warfield, writing in *The Presbyterian*, on May 2, 1904, defined Calvinism as 'religion in its purity.' He continued, 'We have only to conceive of religion in its purity, and that is Calvinism.' Few have had the courage (or audacity) to say it so directly, or the clarity of mind to prove the point. He goes on to ask when it is that one is in the most religious frame of mind and heart? Is it not in the attitude of prayer? And what is the attitude of prayer? Is it not the attitude of 'utter dependence and humble trust?' This is of the essence of

prayer. One bows in prayer because one is in need of God. However, when prayer stops, some people get off their knees and go about their business in a totally different frame of mind, as though it were all up to them, as though they were no longer dependent upon God. And what is Calvinism but a conception of God which requires that one maintain this attitude of prayer, this attitude of dependence and trust, when one gets off of one's knees and begins the other activities of life? Never am I autonomous. Never am I on my own. Never do I find myself in a sphere which excludes God. Life will not divide up into the religious and non-religious. Because God is sovereign over all of life, dependence upon God is unending, and the attitude of prayer ever necessary.

> The Calvinist is the man who is determined to preserve the attitude he takes in prayer in all his thinking, in all his feeling, in all his doing.... Other men are Calvinists on their knees; the Calvinist is the man who is determined that his intellect, and heart, and will shall remain on their knees continually, and only from this attitude think, and feel and act.[1]

So, there is a comprehensiveness about Calvinism that one will not find in other religions or other Christian belief systems. We can see this in two senses. Everything is *for* God, and everything is *through* God. First, all I do, and all everyone does, is to be *for* His glory and according to His command. Second, all I do is to be *through* the strength He gives. Again, God's claim upon me is comprehensive. Likewise, God's control of my life is comprehensive. I am

---

1. B.B. Warfield, *Shorter Writings* I, p. 390.

dependent upon Him at all times. Thus, I am accountable to Him at all times. The much-regretted problem of 'Sunday Christianity,' of people who act one way on Sunday in church and quite another on Monday, will not stand the test of Calvinism. My obligation to Him is comprehensive. My need of Him is comprehensive. I am always under His rule. I am always in His hands. Calvinism, then, is more than a 'religion.' It is a whole 'world and life view.' Abraham Kuyper captured the essence of this outlook when he said,

> There is not an inch in the whole area of human existence of which Christ, the sovereign of all, does not cry, 'It is Mine.'

Kuyper himself is perhaps the ultimate example of a man with a world and life view. Having been trained at Leyden (the Harvard of the Netherlands), he was converted while in the parish ministry through the witness of the older women in his church. His redeemed heart was consumed with the vision of Christ glorified in every sphere. During his lifetime he authored 230 books, edited two newspapers, founded the Free University of Amsterdam, was a member of Parliament, and finally, Prime Minister of the Netherlands. All this was done in addition to his main work, that of theological study, within which he earned recognition as one of the leading theologians of his day. On the occasion of the twenty-fifth anniversary of his editorship of *De Standaard* Kuyper said,

> One desire has been the ruling passion of my life. One high motive has acted like a spur upon my mind and soul.... It is this: That in spite of all worldly opposition, God's holy ordinances shall be established again in the home, in the

school and in the State for the good of the people; to carve as it were into the conscience of the nation the ordinances of the Lord, to which Bible and Creation bear witness, until the nation pays homage again to God.[2]

In many ways this simplifies the Christian life. People seem to have such a hard time understanding what Calvinism is. Actually, it is very simple. It is 'God first,' everywhere. It is life lived from the perspective of 'for God, through God.' It is the attitude which says, Whether I eat or drink or whatever I do, it will all be for the glory of God (1 Cor. 10:31); which says, Apart from Him I can do nothing (John 15:5).

2. Hopeful

Noted historian Carl N. Degler's recently published *In Search of Human Nature* traces the explanations of human nature and consequent behavior in the secular social sciences since 1800 and, especially, since Darwin. He finds that secular discussion has swung back and forth between nature and nurture as explanations for behavior. But what these two poles have in common is far more important than that over which they differ. The common element (surprise!) is determinism. The nurture argument, which has generally been the majority view since 1930, posits an environmental determinism. Why do we behave as we do? The 'nurture' side answers, because of our environment. We were beaten by our father, dominated by our mother, suffered in poverty, lacked education, denied opportunities, etc. That explains our behavior. People are not evil, society is. The key to eliminating evil in the world is to alter the environment. Social change is necessary.

---

2. Abraham Kuyper, *Lectures on Christianity*, p. iii.

The 'nature' argument explains behavior by the nature of things. It posits a genetic determinism. We behave as we do because nature has programmed us the way that it has. This view dominated social thought from roughly 1800 until 1930, and has come into dominance again in just the last few years. The logic of this position led some states in the past to enact policies of enforced castration of those individuals considered genetically inferior, including some criminals, the mentally deficient, and some races. Today, homosexuality is being called a genetic condition, as is alcohol abuse and even all criminal behavior. Genetic flaws or weaknesses are the reasons for all antisocial and destructive behavior. The hope for the future is to be found in genetic experimentation.

The fascinating thing to me is that the most vociferous critic of Calvinism, secular humanistic man, will rail against Calvinism for its doctrine of predestination, yet, when he sits down to describe human behavior, he cannot avoid determinism. He basically poses two alternatives and they're both deterministic! Both destroy human freedom and responsibility. Calvinism, not in spite of, but because of, the doctrine of the eternal decree, establishes the only foundation for human freedom. The *Westminster Confession of Faith* explicitly says this in affirming that God has decreed all things yet He has done so in such a way that 'violence' is not done to the will of the creature, 'nor is the liberty of contingency of second causes taken away, but rather established' (III.2). Because the Reformed faith affirms that God decrees all things, including the free acts of men, it preserves human responsibility and the reality of human choices. It is balanced in a way that no other outlook is or can be.

What difference does this make? It is vital for preserving hope. Are you helpless like the animals are before the forces of nature? Granted, the forces of nature are powerful. The things in one's genes and in one's environment do make a significant impact on one's behavior and choices. But are they determinative? Are they primary? Or is your will? If environment or genes are, indeed you are helpless. You have no choices. And here is the key—there are no solutions, or at least none which are accessible to you. Nothing you do can help you. You are a victim, oppressed by hidden forces which are beyond your power to resist. That is why you get drunk. That is why you are promiscuous. That is why you lose your temper and become violent. That is why you get depressed. You are like one of Pavlov's dogs. The bell rings and you salivate. You are programmed or conditioned to do what you do. What can be done according to the secular schemes? The 'nurture' position leads inevitably to the liberal agenda of massive government intervention for the purpose of correcting society's ills. The 'nature' position leads to a Hitlerian world of eugenics and the elimination of inferior human specimens. Only the Calvinistic view preserves the hope that I can be other than I am. It preserves the reality of human choices and responsibility, while recognizing an all determinative Force is not a force at all but the personal God of the Bible whose help can free us from the greatest powers of nature. I am a drunk, or a homosexual, or a criminal, primarily and determinately, because I *choose* to be such. *I* am responsible. And, by the grace of God, I can choose to be otherwise. It will not do to blame the environment or my genes. I am made in the image of God with the power to choose. There is always hope, with the power that God gives, that I will begin to make right choices.

Realistic

'Unreality in religion is an accursed thing,' says J. I. Packer.[2]
There is no theological tradition as serious about sin as is the
Reformed. While not minimizing the greatness of God's
grace (indeed no other so magnifies the 'amazing grace' of
God), it nevertheless remains realistic about what can be
accomplished in this world to eliminate the effects of sin.
This realism becomes outright skepticism when it comes to
the various utopian and statist schemes for perfecting humanity
and society. Volumes could be written about this subject
alone. But our topic is 'practical piety,' and so we will remind
ourselves of the peace of mind that comes through a realistic
view of evil as it touches us personally.

First, the Reformed faith is realistic about *sanctification*.
Thousands of Christians have been tyrannized by the idea
that they should not struggle with sin. They have been told,
by those who fail to realize the pervasiveness of sin, that if
they had either a special experience or enough faith they
would eliminate the presence of sin and the struggle that goes
with it. I call this tyranny because it is unrealistic and
unachievable. People have driven themselves almost mad
trying to find the key to the effortless Christian life.

The Reformed understanding of the *ordo salutis* is a
beautifully sensible and balanced grasp of things which
belong together but are different. Justification is not
sanctification. The former is a declaration, while sanctification
is a process. Regeneration is not sanctification. The former
frees us from the enslaving power of sin, while the latter
addresses the ongoing need of mortifying the sin that remains.
We are passive as God regenerates, we are justified the
moment we exercise faith, but we must 'work out'

2. J.I. Packer, *Knowing God*, IVP, p. 228.

sanctification because 'God is at work' in us.

Second, the Reformed faith is realistic about *suffering*. Silly 'health and wealth' gospels of this and previous generations imagine that life can be pain-free. Superficial, untrained Christians can conclude that because 'God is love,' and we are His children, He does not want us to suffer. People accustomed to thinking this way can be utterly devastated when the inevitable tragedy does come, as well as disillusioned and angry with God. 'Why would He allow this to happen?' they cry. Again, the Reformed faith promotes a much more realistic and Biblical set of expectations. It takes the effects of Adam's sin and God's judgments more seriously—this is, after all, a fallen world. Moreover, the dregs of sin that remain in the hearts of the regenerate are so deeply rooted that they rarely come out without suffering—'whom the Lord loves He disciplines.'

Third, the Reformed faith is realistic about the *need of law*. The antinomians promote a version of the Christian life that is free from the constraints of law. Again, they fail to take seriously the effects of sin. The eradicating of sin is so difficult and incomplete in this life that even the redeemed heart needs objective criteria by which to order conduct. The saints need limits. The saints need guidance. The saints need law if they are to live according to the will of God. The place of law in the Christian life is certainly open to abuse. Legalism is always a danger, but carnality and subjective rationalizations of sin are also a danger. Life without limits seems appealing. In reality, it brings moral disaster.

The Reformed faith is sometimes accused of being a joyless, austere, harsh faith. It gets tagged with these labels because it is not afraid to tell the truth. Some prefer to live in a fantasy world, free from pain and struggle and limits. One can live with that outlook for a while and talk Pollyanna-like about how wonderful life is. But eventually, the fantasy meets reality, and then the pain is immeasurably worse, compounded by disappointment and even a sense of betrayal. We maintain that the joy is greater and the peace is more consistent when one faces the sometimes bitter facts about life in a world under the curse of God. Life *is* tough. Life *is* a struggle. We deal daily with sickness and death. Christ does not deliver us from pain, but rather enables us to deal with our pain. 'Unreality towards God is the wasting disease of much modern Christianity,' says Packer.[3] The Reformed faith helps us to be real.

Balanced

Everywhere we look in the contemporary church we see truth that is out-of-balance. Elements of truth are seized upon, isolated, magnified, and thereby distorted. Partial-truths are proclaimed as though they were the whole story and, as Packer says, 'a half-truth presented as the whole truth is a complete untruth.'[4] The Christian faith has been warped out of recognition. The cure for what ails the church may be found in the careful, balanced answers that the Reformed faith gives to the major questions we face.

First, it strikes the right balance between *God's part and our part*. We have commented on this several times already. Is sanctification a work of God or a work of man? It is both. We avoid the passivity of those who make it a work of God alone and the frustration and failure of those who make it a work of man alone. Does God save or does man save? Both. God saves through our use of the ordained means of grace.

---

2. J.I. Packer, *Knowing God*, IVP, p. 228.
3. J. I. Packer, *A Quest For Godliness*, Crossway, p. 165.

We avoid the fatalism of those who say it is all up to God and the manipulative practices of those who say it is all up to us. We pray, preach the gospel, and wait for God to work.

Second, it strikes the right balance between the *objective and the subjective*, between fact and feeling, between knowledge and experience.

Look at the following areas: Are we under *law* or under *grace*? Both. We avoid the legalism of those who live under the law as a means of justification by clearly affirming that one is justified by faith; and we avoid the carnality of those who reject law and make grace and 'the leading of the Holy Spirit' a license for sin.

Is *assurance* easy to get or difficult? It is both. By insisting that the 'signs of grace' must be present in the lives of the believer, we avoid the presumptuousness of those who cheapen grace, making assurance too easy, promoting carnality among believers and false assurance among the self-deceived; and we avoid the mistake of making assurance too hard, driving sensitive saints to despair and denying many others the peace of heart which they ought to have, since 'these things were written that you might *know* you have eternal life.'

Finally, is *guidance* found through the Spirit or through the word? Both. The extreme fanatics who, on the one hand, claim the direct inspiration of the Spirit, words from the Lord, infallible impulses; and of the deists, who, on the other hand, gag God and won't allow Him to speak, are avoided. The Spirit leads us, not through new revelation, but by illuminating the given word and our circumstances. Thus, the authority and finality of the Scripture is protected, as is also the reality of a living relationship with Christ.

In closing, we come back again to the profound wisdom of B.B. Warfield. In an address delivered to the PCUS General

Assembly as it convened at the First Presbyterian Church in Savannah, Georgia, in May, 1909, Warfield said, 'Calvinism is evangelicalism in its pure and only stable expression.' Evangelicalism in its 'purity' is an evangelicalism that magnifies the saving work of God. No expression of evangelicalism does so as clearly and boldly as that which proclaims the doctrine of man's total inability, his 'total depravity', and total dependence upon God for salvation. Others confuse the issue by giving some power of response to the natural man. Calvinism will have none of it. Calvinism debases man, but by so doing, it exalts the saving work of Christ and the gracious love of God as no other form of belief can.

Evangelicalism is most stable in its Calvinistic expression because only then is it completely free of the poison of rationalism. The 'rationalist' is one who exalts human reason over God's revelation. An evangelicalism that rejects the doctrines of predestination and election sows the seeds of its own destruction. Because there are so many texts which clearly teach the sovereignty of God, those who reject this teaching must 'rationalize' these texts away. Whether they realize it or not, reason, logic, or common sense comes to be preferred to Scripture's teaching. Once that happens with regard to predestination, the door is open to explaining away other clear texts of Scripture that don't suit one's tastes. The Calvinist alone is willing to say, 'I don't understand it completely, but I see it in Scripture, and so, I believe it.' Scripture remains normative and so, evangelicalism remains 'stable.' Calvinists who minimize or even hide their Calvinistic distinctives should ponder this closely. Evangelicalism, that great movement of conservative doctrine and missionary

5. B.B. Warfield, *Calvin Memorial Addresses*, p. 228.

endeavor, is only pure, and only remains pure, when it remains true to its Calvinistic roots.

The Reformed faith is comprehensive, hopeful, realistic, balanced, and evangelical. It is a breath of fresh air in a crazy, mixed-up church. It gives us a framework within which to understand our *identity* as humble sinners saved by grace; our *experiences* in a fallen world—of suffering, struggle, doubt, duty, and guidance; and our *duties* of worship, prayer, and witness. It is the religion of the Bible in its most pure, practical, and stable form.

Persons Index

Ames, William 9
Anderson, John 85
Anselm 88
Aquinas, Thomas 34
Augustine 9, 11, 34, 48, 67, 92, 139, 167
Barnhouse, Dr Donald 53-4
Beza, Theodore 9
Bradford, John 38
Bright, Bill 84
Bunyan, John 84
Calvin, John 9, 11, 13, 16, 34, 118, 119, 125, 139, 159
Carey, William 66, 76, 84
Cecil, Richard 85
Cohen, Mickey 130
Cotton, John 9
Cranmer, Thomas 9
Dallimore, arnold 85
Darwin, Charles 172
Defoe, Daniel 65
Degler, Carl N. 172
Duff, Alexander 85
Duncan, 'Rabbi' 99
Edwards, Jonathan 33, 34, 84, 85
Fergammo, Vince 50
Ferguson, Sinclair, 25
George, II King 29
Goodwin, Thomas 9
Haden, Ben 53
Harris, Howell 84
Havergal, Francis Ridley 64
Hodge, Charles 58
Hooker, Thomas 9
Hooper, John 9
James II, King 65
Kennedy, D. James 84
Knox, John 9
Kuyper, Abraham 171-2
Latimer, Hugh 9
Livingstone, David 85
Luther, Martin 9, 34, 92, 118
McCheyne, Robert Murray 84, 139
Machen, J. Gresham 49
Moffat, Robert 84
Moody, Dwight 33
Morrison, Robert 84
Muggeridge, Malcolm 59-60
Murray, Ian 42, 66
Murray, John 90
Newton, John 85
Owen, John 9
Packer, J.I. 70, 84, 96, 118, 121, 166, 175, 177
Pal, Krishna 66
Paton, John G. 41, 42, 85
Richardson, Dr John 47
Richardson, R.J. 47
Ridley, Nicholas 9
Rowlands, Daniel 84
Rylands, John Sr. 76
Ryle, J.C. 96

181

Schaeffer, Henry F. 32
Scott, Thomas 85
Sibbes, Richard 131
Spafford, Horatius 63
Sproul, R.C. 11
Spurgeon, Charles Haddon 9, 23, 84, 149
Still, William 82
Stott, John 95-6
Tennant, Gilbert 84
Tennant, Williams 84
Thatcher, Margaret 152

Van Puffelen, Anton 41
Venn, Henry 85
von Braun, Dr Werner 167
Warfield, Benjamin B. 34, 41-2, 96, 169, 178-9
Watts, Isaac 26
Wesleys (Charles & John) 33, 84
Whitefield, George 33, 84, 85
Williams, Roger 9
Wilson, John 85

Biblical Persons Index

Abraham 20, 21, 65, 123
Adam 43, 176
Daniel 143-44, 148
David 123, 140, 141, 143, 156
Demas 110
Elijah 148
Esau 20, 21
Gabriel 148
Gamaliel 164
Herod 11
Hezekiah 141, 143
Job 44, 57
John 59, 110, 114, 117, 142
Joseph 10, 51
Jude 105
Luke 142
Moses 21, 30, 123, 148
Nehemiah 144-5
Nicodemus 73

Noah 11
Paul 12, 13, 17, 20-23, 25, 31-33, 35-7, 48-50, 54-62, 67, 79-80, 82, 91, 97-9, 102-05, 110-11, 117, 126, 130, 133, 148, 150, 158, 163-4
Isaac 20, 21
Isaiah 23, 122
Peter 11, 58-9, 110, 117, 123, 142
Ishmael 20, 21
Pharaoh 21, 22, 51
Jacob 20, 21
Pilate 11, 44
James 58, 111, 145, 146, 148, 160
Potiphar's wife 51
Jeremiah 11, 141, 143
Rebekah 20
Samuel 123
Sarah 65
Timothy 13

Subject Index

Anglican/Episcopal 9

Antinomy 70, 75-6

Arminian(ism) 76, 83, 102, 117, 149

Baptist 9, 84

Calvinism 9, 10, 14, 16, 27-31, 64, 69, 76-7, 84-5, 169-173, 179

Calvinist(ic) 9, 15, 23, 26, 30-1, 38, 52, 66-7, 76-7, 84-5, 92, 108, 137-8, 147, 149, 170, 174, 179-80

Campus Crusade for Christ 84

Church of England 29, 33, 84

Church of Scotland 29, 151

Congregational 9

Contentment 60-4, 80

Covenanters 65

Determinism 172-4

Election/Predestination 13, 15, 20-1, 23, 25, 31, 43, 69-74, 76-7, 103, 106, 108, 117, 137, 179

Evangelism Explosion 84

Hope 64-8

Huguenot 15

Human depravity 11-12, 19, 26, 31, 37, 45, 93, 169

Indians 30

Larger Catechism, 11,

Lutherans 9

Mexicans 30

Perseverance 106-8, 119

Pharisee(ism) 88, 128, 134, 164

Presbyterian (churches) 9, 15, 41-2, 65, 84, 92, 152, 155, 161, 179

Protestant(ism) 9, 84

Puritans 15, 36, 66, 84, 102, 114, 125, 131

Reformation 84

Reformed/Reformers 9, 15, 29-30, 37, 65, 69, 77, 88, 93, 99, 102, 108, 118, 121, 123, 125, 129, 133, 138-9, 152, 157, 162-3, 167-8, 173, 175-7, 180

Reformed churches 9, 128

Shorter Catechism 10

Southern Baptist Convention 9

Sovereignty of God 10-11, 12-14, 19, 22, 24, 26, 31, 34, 42, 45-6, 51-2, 55, 60, 62, 64, 67, 69, 73, 76, 78, 82, 83, 85, 88, 103, 106, 108, 147, 149, 152, 163-64, 169-70, 179

Spanish Inquisition 65

Westminster Confession of Faith 10, 13, 29, 125, 157, 173

Wycliffe Bible Translators 45

Scripture
References

Genesis
6:5 11
12:3 123
45:8 51
50:20 10, 51

Exodus
17:11 148

Numbers
12:3 30

1Chron
29:10-13 141

Nehemiah
1:3 144-5
1:4-7 145

Job
1:5-22 53
1:20-21 57

Psalms
16 123
19 132
19:10 128
23 155
23:2-3 155
25:8 156
25:9 156
25: 12 156
119 128
119:9 158
119:11 158
119:97 128
119:105 158

119:105 126
119:111 126
139 55
139:8 55

Proverbs
11:14 161
12:15 161
13:10 161
15:22 161
19:20 161
20:18 161
21:1 83
24:6 161

Ecclesiastes
9:3 12

Isaiah
1:18 17
5:20 122
6:5 143
6:9 75
37:16 141
45:7 10

Jeremiah
9:23-24 35
17:9 12, 162
32:17-19 142

Ezekiel
18:4 43

Daniel
9:4-11 143-44
9:22, 23 148
10:12ff 148

Hosea
4:6 16

Jonah
2:9 12, 37

Matthew
5:17-19 124
5:17-22 121
5:21ff 125
5:29-30 97
6:6 140
6:9 140
6:10 140
7:15-20 117
7:22, 23 111
10:29-30 10
11:25-27 71
11:25-30 69
11:28-30 71
11:29 30
13:20 109
13:24-30 109
28:19-20 70

Mark
4:3-9 75
4:3-20 75
4:10-13 75
4:13-20 75
4:13 75
7:19 130
9:23 65

Luke
3:21 160
5:16 160
6:12 160

7:47 26
9:18 160
9:28-29 160
11:2ff 160
11:9-10 147
13 44
13:5 45

John
1:12-13 72
1:13 12
3:7-8 73
3:8 12
3:19-20 12, 37
5:46 123
6:35 73
6:36-37 74
6:44 12, 74
6:65 74
8:31 108
8:56 123
10:27 105
10:29 105
14:13-14 148
15:5 89, 172
15:7 148
15:16 12, 36, 148
17:17 126

Acts
1:14 151
2:23 11, 48
2:31 123
2:39 13
2:47 13
2:42 151
3:24 123
4:24 142
4:28 11

5:31 13
5:41 59
11:18 13
13:48 13, 77
14:22 58
16:14 13
16:35-40 163
17:1ff. 164
18:10 82-3
20:27 17
23:6 164
25:11 163

Romans
1:16 81
1:30-31 25
3:10-12 12
3:20 128
3:31 131
4:19 65
4:20-21 65
5:3-6 59
6:1-11 87
6:4 89
6:5-6 89
6:11 95
6:14 90
6:17-18 90
7 97-9
7:7–8:4 87
7:14 125
7:15 97, 98
7:19 98
7:22 97
7:24 98
7:25 98-9
8 48, 99, 102
8:1-4 121
8:4 126

8:12-14 159
8:12-17 101
8:13 97
8:15-16 118
8:17 48
8:18 49
8:23 49
8:24-25 49
8:26 49
8:26-39 41
8:28 10, 49, 55
8:28-39 101
8:29 103
8:30 50, 103
8:31-35 104
8:35 104-05
8:37-39 104-5
9–11 20, 75
9:1–11:36 19
9:6-7 20
9:11-13 21
9:14 21
9:15-16 21
9:16 75
9:18 21
9:19 22
9:20-22 22
9 22
10:9 22
10:12 22
10:13 23, 75, 114
11:5 21
11:26 21
11:33-36 9, 19, 23, 169
11:36 169

13:8-10 127
14 130

1Corinthians
1:18-31 29
1:18 32
1:20 32
1:21 32
1:22-23 33
1:26-29 31, 33
1:29-31 35
1:30 35, 89
1:31 12, 35
2–3 37
2:1 79
2:2 80
2:3 79
2:3-5 33
2:4 79
2:5 33, 79
2:14 37, 82, 97, 117
2:16 159
4:7 37
6:10 111
7 131
7:27ff 131
8–10 130
9:27 97
10:31 172
15:10 37, 39

2Corinthians
3:18 91
4:2 82
5:17 91
6:14ff 131
12:1-10 53

12:2 55
12:7-8 56
12:9 56, 80
12:9-10 60
12:10 60, 64
13:5 117

Galatians
1:15 163
3:8 123
3:24 128
3:29 123
4:11 110
5:13 111, 131
5:17 98
5:21 111
5:22-23 92
5:24 97

Ephesians
1–2 25
1 20
1:1-14 19
1:3–3:21 25
1:4-6 25
1:4-5 13
1:6 25
1:7 89
1:7-8 25-6
1:11 10
1:11-12 25
1:17-18 148
2:1 25
2:1-3 12
2:5 12
2:8 36
2:8-9 12, 104
5:18-19 159
6:11-18 97

Philippians
1:9 48
2:13-14 88
3:4-8 163
3:12 99
4 67
4:6 150
4:11-12 61
4:13 61

Colossians
1:9 148
2:16-23 130
2:20-22 130
3:5 97, 129
3:6 107
3:8 97
3:10 97
3:16 159
4:3 148
4:14 1110

1Thessalonians
4:6 111
5:16-18 57
5:23 91

2Thessalonians
2:13 13

1Timothy
3:15 133
4:1-4 130

2Timothy
1:9 13
2:1-24 97
2:12 108
3:16 126, 159
3:17 159
4:2-4 82
4:10 110

Philemon
24 110

Hebrews
2:14-15 90
4:1 107
6:4-5 110
6:4-6 107
10:26-31 111-2
10:26 110
10:26-27 107
10:31 107
10:36 108
12:6-11 58

James
1:2-4 58
1:5 160
2:26 111
4:1-10 137
4:2 146
4:3 145
4:8-10 146
5:16 148-9
5:17-18 148

1 Peter
1:5 108
1:6-7 58-9
1:22 126

2 Peter
1:10 117
2:20-21 110

1 John
1:6 106
1:7 114
1:8 110
1:9 114
1:10 110
2:3-11 101
2:3 116
2:3ff 113

2:4 110
2:5 116
2:6 110
2:9 110
2:15 115
2:19 108
2:22 115
2:29 115
3:6-8 115
3:9 90
3: 9-10 115
3:14 116
3:18-19 116
3:24 116
4:7 115
4:13 116
4:15 115
4:19 12; 36
4:20 115
5:1 116
5:2 116
5:4 91, 108, 116
5:13 113
5:14 148
5:18 91, 116

Jude
25 105

Terry Johnson is the Senior Minister of the historic Independent Presbyterian Church in Savannah, Georgia, USA. In 1993 he was named the convenor and then chairman of the PCA General Assembly committee on Psalm-singing. Among the fruit of their labours was the *Trinity Psalter*, of which he was the editor and compiler. He has also published *Leading in Worship*, a source-book for Presbyterian ministers, and *The Family Worship Book*, a resource book for family devotions (the latter published by Christian Focus Publications). He is married to the former Emily Billings and they have five children.